M000079861

FAMILY WALKS

in

THE WEALD

of

KENT & SUSSEX

Sally and Clive Cutter

Scarthin Books, Cromford, Derbyshire 1994.

FAMILY WALKS
in the WEALD of KENT and SUSSEX

Family Walks Series
General Editor: Norman Taylor

———————

THE COUNTRY CODE

Enjoy the countryside and respect its life and work
Guard against all risk of fire
Fasten all gates
Keep your dogs under close control
Keep to public paths across farmland
Use gates and stiles to cross fences, hedges and walls
Leave livestock, crops and machinery alone
Take your litter home
Help to keep all water clean
Protect wildlife, plants and trees
Take special care on country roads
Make no unnecessary noise

———————

Published 1992

Phototypesetting, printing by Higham Press Ltd., Shirland, Derbyshire

ISBN 0 907758 51 7.

FOOTBRIDGE NEAR ROTHERFIELD (Route 5)

1

MAP OF THE AREA

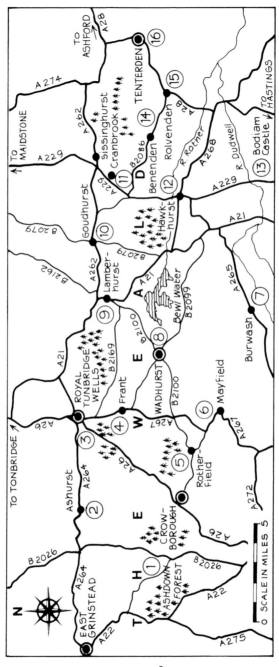

CONTENTS

Introduction

The Weald of Kent and Sussex

For the modern visitor the Weald of Kent and Sussex is fairly easily accessible, full of interest and very beautiful. It is also very old. As children clamber over the famous Wellington Rocks near Tunbridge Wells, parents may reflect that this sandstone outcrop, one of many in the region, dates back about a hundred million years and was formed as a result of sedimentation at the bottom of a great lake that used to cover nearly the whole of South East England!

During the last Ice Age the lake was frozen, later withdrawing to leave an undulating hollow roughly bordered by the North and South Downs. Thick forests then covered a large part of the area, becoming known by the Saxons as Andreaswald, a small remainder being the lovely Ashdown Forest, where children will undoubtedly need no further invitation when confronted by a neat wooden sign pointing the way towards the wonderful Poohsticks Bridge.

Agriculture eventually followed a lengthy period of prosperity derived from the iron and cloth industries, making the Weald into the charming mixture of farmland and woods that can be seen today.

Family Walks

The forests of the Weald were once so thick that the coast of Sussex was cut off from Kent and the rest of the country, only being approachable from the sea. Now of course the two counties are linked by an excellent road system and a vast network of footpaths, giving the public an opportunity to enhance a visit to one of many charming villages by also plunging into the surrounding countryside.

Children will be enthralled by many farm animals which can be seen on most of the walks, and whether simply curious in passing or perhaps enjoying the satisfaction of a growing knowledge on the subject, the family can share the pleasures of suddenly coming across a splendid array of wildflowers, butterflies and birds, as well as regularly being surprised by yet another breathtaking panorama. Rolling green pastures and peaceful woods seem to beckon the explorer, who is also bound to enjoy treading the paths through the enchanting valleys of the River Medway near Ashurst, the River Dudwell which was harnessed at one point on its course by Rudyard Kipling to provide electricity for his home of Bateman's, and the River Rother which flows leisurely past the magnificent grounds of the highly evocative Bodiam Castle.

4

Whether a choice is made from this collection of walks either for convenience or perhaps in search of some specific treasure such as the far-reaching views around Mayfield or the gorgeous sea of pink orchard blossom seen in Spring from the heights of Goudhurst, or whether a more systematic approach is taken by moving eastwards, following the order of the routes in a rough zig-zag from Ashdown Forest to the Ancient Cinque Port of Tenterden, headquarters of the cherished Kent and East Sussex Railway, the experience should prove most rewarding for both young and old, adding a new dimension to the phrase "fun for the whole family".

Dedication

To our families and friends.

The Authors

Sally and Clive Cutter live in Kent, where they enjoy exploring the beautiful countryside. This book, which was written by Clive and illustrated by Sally, who also provided the maps and photographs, is the result of their rambles through the Weald.

Acknowledgements

Thanks to Joan and Dorothy for their company on many of the walks.

THE PATH TO POOH BRIDGE

5

Symbols used on route maps

→ — → — → — → Route (right of way unless otherwise stated)

· Footpath (**not** en route)

– – – – – – – – – – – – – Track

═══════════════ Road

+ + + + + + + + + + + + Railway

River

Stream

Village

Woodland

Bridge

Lake   ○ Pond

■ Building(s)

+ Church

Steep Slope

CP Car Park

② etc.   Number corresponds with route description

Route 1 4 miles

Poohsticks Bridge

Outline   Pooh Car Park ~ Poohsticks Bridge ~ Marsh Green ~ Pooh Car Park.

Summary   The sign to Poohsticks Bridge will have children scampering excitedly ahead through the woods, while the lovely variegated hedgerows bordering the adjacent farmland, which is dotted with giant oaks and at times quietly grazing horses, will help to release adults from the cares of modern life, leaving them free to absorb the magical atmosphere of the place with the unhindered spontaneity of the youngsters. Sweeping views over the valley and the Ashdown Forest on the opposite slopes make the second part of the route very relaxing in spite of numerous stiles, several possibly rather too high for the comfort of the elderly, although, as with some of the little children, sheer enjoyment may tap unknown resources of energy and mobility.

Attractions   Where better for children to play poohsticks than the original Poohsticks Bridge? The Ashdown Forest Trust, the present Lord of the Manor, advises children to bring their own sticks and pine cones, but this is surely a small price to pay for admission to a world of fantasy. There is a friendly air along the wide, well-signposted paths, and visitors will often exchange greetings as they pass, mindful no doubt of the happiness brought to millions of children throughout the world by the charming adventures of Winnie-The-Pooh and his friends, written about 60 years ago by A. A. Milne at Cotchford Farm near Hartfield.

Ashdown Forest, known by the Romans as the Forest of Anderida, used to extend over most of South East England. Agricultural development was started by the Saxons who called it Andreaswald. Then, in the reign of King Edward III (14th Century), it was called Silva Regalis, which meant the royal hunting ground. During the iron industry of the 16th Century, largely for the production of weapons to arm the fleet, the area was threatened by such a shortage of trees, which were cut for charcoal to smelt the ore, that the Tudors were afraid there wouldn't be enough timber left to make the ships! Eventually the iron industry moved to the north where coal was used instead.

Today the forest stretches over 140,000 acres, this particular walk touching its northern border. Striking outcrops of yellow gorse can be seen in Spring as well as hardy clusters of primroses and sweet violets flourishing beside the hedgerows, while delicate white wood anemones

continued on page 10

7

Route 1

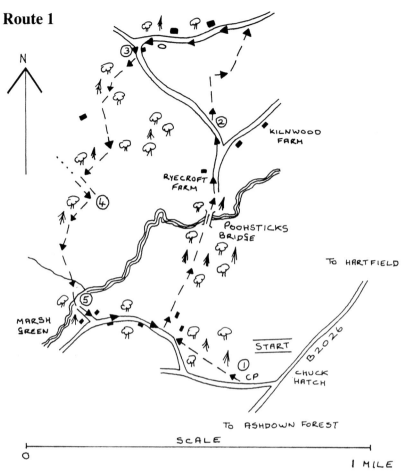

N

KILNWOOD FARM

RYECROFT FARM

POOHSTICKS BRIDGE

TO HARTFIELD

MARSH GREEN

START

B 2026

CP

CHUCK HATCH

TO ASHDOWN FOREST

SCALE

0   1 MILE

PRIMROSE (yellow early Spring)

Route 1
Poohsticks Bridge   4 miles

START   *at the Pooh Car Park (O.S. Pathfinder 1248 G.R.472331), about two hundred yards along Marsh Green turnoff from B2026 (near Chuck Hatch).*

ROUTE
1. *Follow sign to Pooh Bridge downhill through wood. Pass between wooden barrier into lane and after about fifty yards follow signposted path to the right, continuing downhill to cross Poohsticks Bridge. Proceed uphill along path, continuing as it leads into a lane bending towards the left. Keep left at a fork in the lane.*
2. *After about a hundred yards cross over a stile into a field on the right. Follow left-hand boundary around field, leaving via a stile beside a gate. Bearing diagonally towards the right continue uphill through another field, crossing over another stile and turning left into a lane. Follow lane to a T-junction with another lane.*
3. *Turn left and after about twenty yards cross a stile into a field on the right. Continue along right-hand boundary, crossing over a stile in the corner before proceeding along path beside a hedge. Cross over another stile and continue straight downhill in the direction of sign to Marsh Green. Cross stile into another field and proceed along right-hand boundary. Cross another stile and turn left into a track indicated by footpath sign.*
4. *On reaching a gate, turn right and follow signposted footpath. Cross a stile and continue along right-hand boundary of a field. Cross another stile and cross through another field bearing diagonally to the left. At a point halfway down opposite hedgerow cross another stile beside a telegraph pole. Continue downhill along path, bearing diagonally towards the left. Cross a small bridge and then, after a further fifty yards, cross a stile immediately followed by a longer bridge.*
5. *Continue along path as it leads into a driveway. On reaching a T-junction, turn left into a lane, proceeding uphill past turnoff on left to Poohsticks Bridge, and retrace steps to car park.*

ACCESS BY BUS
To Hartfield from Tunbridge Wells and East Grinstead.

are a picture beneath the trees. In May there is a profusion of hawthorn blossom and then later clematis and heavy-scented honeysuckle.

Back at the Poohsticks Bridge turnoff, towards the end of the route, children may want to dart off for another quick game of poohsticks, although parents may illustrate the consequences of over-indulgence by reminding them that Pooh Bear got stuck in Rabbit's hole after greedily gorging too much honey! Not to be accused of spoiling the fun, as well as further indulging themselves, they could then take the children to Pooh Corner, a fascinating shop in Hartfield, or perhaps to see the inspirational setting of The Enchanted Place, Galleon's Lap and Roo's Sandy Pit, about half a mile further south along the B2026, reached from a car park called simply "Piglet's".

Refreshments   A picnic on the route or a pub in nearby Hartfield or perhaps an ice cream from Pooh Corner.

ON THE MEDWAY

Ashurst

Outline   Ashurst ~ Jessups Farm ~ Hale Court Farm ~ Blackham Court ~ Lodgefield Farm ~ Ashurst.

Summary   Passing mainly through rich, rolling farmland, this walk follows part of the Sussex Border Path, with lovely sweeping views to the right over the valley of the River Medway, before joining a short section of the long-distance Weald Way (which runs from Gravesend, over the North Downs, across the Weald and through the Ashdown Forest, eventually coming out at Eastbourne!) Perhaps already enthralled by the sight of cattle grazing in the fields, further opportunities being regularly available along the way, children will be delighted by the neat wooden footbridge over the river Grom, a tributary of the Medway, where the family may wish to linger as they watch the relaxing flow of the water and, on sunny days, the many butterflies and dragonflies dipping on its surface. Crossing another stream and then the gently meandering River Medway, the route forges into East Sussex past the picturesque Hale Court Farm to reach the quiet winding driveway of Blackham Court. From the pretty gardens of the lovely buildings further up the hill, including a converted oasthouse and also a fine example of tile-hanging and weatherboarding, as well as the clockhouse stables of Lodgefield Farm, the route sweeps down into the inviting green bowl of the Medway valley back to Ashurst.

Attractions   The ash tree was held sacred by the Saxons. "Hurst" was their word for wood. And so the name Ashurst. The mill and pond near the start of the walk in Ashurst Hill are a vestige of the iron industry, cannons being produced in 1609.

A fascinating change of vantage points should provide more than adequate compensation for several rather steep hills on this route and in hot weather further compensation may be derived from several welcome stretches of shade, especially the tree-lined section of the Sussex Border Path after the climb from Jessups Farm and then later the cool woodland at the start of the driveway to Blackham Court.

In Spring vast banks of blackthorn blossom bordering some of the fields may seem like deep drifts of snow and children may be pleasantly startled by the sudden flapping of a wood pigeon, the brash cry of a magpie or the extraordinary call of the colourful pheasant. This is a birdwatcher's paradise and binoculars may be handy. Also in Spring, on

continued on page 14

11

Route 2

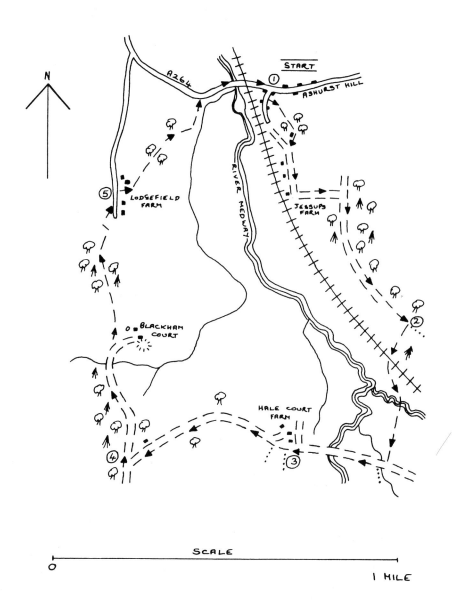

N

START

A264

ASHURST HILL

RIVER MEDWAY

①

⑤ LODGEFIELD FARM

JESSUPS FARM

②

BLACKHAM COURT

HALE COURT FARM

③

④

SCALE

O

1 MILE

12

Route 2
Ashurst

3½ miles

START   *at the corner of Ashurst Hill (A264) and the signposted road leading to Ashurst Station (O.S. Pathfinder 1248 G.R.507389) (at the Bald Faced Stag). Parking in road leading to station.*

ROUTE

1. *From Ashurst Hill (at the Bald Faced Stag) walk along station road for about twenty yards before crossing a stile to the left. Proceed uphill through a field, bearing diagonally towards the right. Pass through a gate in top right corner and, after a further fifty yards, pass through a second gate. Continue along left border of a garden. Pass through another gate and bear left as path joins a track. Continue past Jessups Farm and then turn left, proceeding uphill along track (indicated as Sussex Border Path). At the top of the hill turn right. Proceed downhill along another track, crossing a stile beside a gate at the bottom. Continue along same track as it keeps to the left border of a field. Pass through a gateway and continue downhill.*

2. *Turn right at indicated Sussex Border Path East, proceeding downhill through a field. Pass through a gate, continue beneath the railway line and then pass through a second gate. Bearing left, follow path through a field. Cross a wooden footbridge (River Grom) and, bearing right, continue through field. Turn right into a track (indicated Weald Way) and cross a bridge. Proceed straight along track, crossing another bridge (River Medway). Continue along track.*

3. *As track swings to the right (just before Hale Court Farm), proceed straight ahead, crossing two stiles within ten yards of each other. Keeping to the right edge of a field, proceed for about fifty yards before passing through a gateway on the right. After a further twenty yards pass through second gateway, continuing straight through a field. Cross a stile in top right corner and turn left, proceeding uphill along winding concrete track, passing through two gateways before eventually reaching a T-junction at the top.*

4. *Turn right and follow indicated driveway to Blackham Court. Just past a small bridge, as driveway swings right into Blackham Court, leave the track and continue straight on, up a grassy slope. On reaching a hedgerow, bear left and continue uphill, keeping hedgerow on the right. Pass through a gate and between fences. Continue along left boundary of a field, leaving at the far left corner through a gate on the left. Turn right, proceeding along border of a field before passing through a gate into a lane.*

5. *After ten yards descend steps on the right (indicated by footpath sign), leading to Lodgefield Farm. Continue down a concrete track and through a gate into a field. Cross field diagonally towards the left. Cross a stile into another field and continue downhill, keeping to left boundary. At the bottom cross over a small gully into another field on the left, proceeding along the right boundary. Cross a stile and turn right (WITH CAUTION) into A264. Continue CAREFULLY beneath railway bridge and retrace steps to car.*

ACCESS BY BUS AND TRAIN
To Ashurst from East Grinstead and Tunbridge Wells by bus, or by train from East Croydon and Crowborough.

---

the banks of the tinkling streams and rivers, a shock of lilac cuckoo flowers may be seen, a common British flower, its blossom said to celebrate the arrival of the cuckoo, while in Summer the delicious red of poppies, the soft purple of thistle flowers and the bright clumps of yellow ragwort colour the landscape. Also in abundance, near the water, the varying shades of pink Indian Balsam flowers can be seen, with their distinctive, beautifully-shaped petals.

As well as the occasional rabbit bolting across a track or field, children may enjoy seeing horses in wooden-fenced paddocks at Hale Court Farm or perhaps near the old manor house of Blackham Court. The nearby moated enclosure, now a tennis court and pool, was once the site of a priory. Excavations have revealed pottery fragments dating back to the 13th Century.

From the impressive heights of Lodgefield Farm there is a wonderful view over the valley, a picture of tranquillity. Three squat concrete pillboxes near the river, from which soldiers watched the skies for enemy aircraft, are perhaps a gentle reminder that this should never be taken for granted. Halfway down the hill, in the shady corner of a grassy field, a leisurely picnic might prove so enjoyable that it goes down in family history!

Refreshments   At the Bald Faced Stag or a picnic along the way.

Wellington Rocks and Toad Rock

Outline   Tunbridge Wells Common ~ Victoria Grove ~ Wellington Rocks ~ Rusthall Common ~ Toad Rock ~ Tunbridge Wells Common.

Summary   The charm of Tunbridge Wells is quite hypnotic. In fact there is such a wealth of attractions in the town that the visitor could easily be sidetracked from exploring the surrounding countryside, which itself is simply enchanting. From the picturesque footpath through Tunbridge Wells Common and the wonders of Wellington Rocks, guaranteed to delight any youngster, to the equally inspiring Toad Rock on Rusthall Common, there is plenty to see and do for all the family. A picnic may be an ideal choice at one of several perfect spots, or alternatively there is a wide choice of pubs and tearooms in Tunbridge Wells, providing a most hospitable welcome back for the tired and happy wanderers.

Attractions   The Pantiles in Tunbridge Wells was developed and began to gain in popularity soon after 1606, when Lord North discovered The Chalybeate Spring which produced iron water, thought to have special healing properties. Many visitors, including royalty and aristocracy, were drawn to the area to take full advantage both of the medicinal water and also the beautiful and peaceful setting, although later visitors were perhaps equally keen on the growing social scene. A fascinating historical tour called A Day At The Wells, presided over by well-known dandy and Master of Ceremonies, Beau Nash, provides the modern visitor with a detailed insight into the way of life in the 18th Century. A special Walkman commentary is also available for children.

Other compelling attractions in this interesting town include The Corn Exchange, originally built as a theatre by the dancer Sarah Baker in 1802 and now a tempting Speciality Food Hall, and also the nearby Sussex Square, with its handmade fashion, art and craft.

The walk leads across Tunbridge Wells Common, passing the lovely Victoria Grove where, in the 19th Century, local residents planted elms, sycamores and lime trees in honour of Queen Victoria, a regular visitor to the town. Next on the route are the Wellington Rocks, the sort of place that will leave treasured memories in the minds of children for the rest of their lives. Formed about a hundred million years ago, these rocks were created by gradual sedimentation on the floor of the Wealden Lake, which was so huge it covered all of South East England, the Straits of Dover and Belgium! Here children can let their imaginations run to

continued on page 18

Route 3

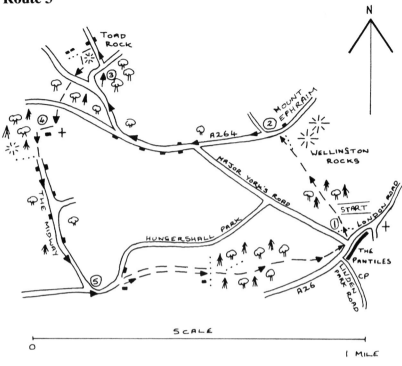

SCALE

0   1 MILE

WELLINGTON ROCKS

Route 3

Wellington Rocks and Toad Rock   3 miles

START   *at the corner of Major York's Road and London Road in Tunbridge Wells (opposite the Swan Hotel) (O.S. Pathfinder 1248 G.R.580387), approached by London Road (A26). Parking in car park off Linden Park Road, behind the Pantiles.*

ROUTE

1. *From the corner of Major York's Road and London Road follow tarmac footpath diagonally to the right leading uphill through Tunbridge Wells Common. At a fork in the path just past Wellington Rocks, take the left tarmac path to reach Mount Ephraim.*

2. *Cross over Mount Ephraim (A264) (WITH CAUTION) and turn left, following a pavement path for about a quarter of a mile, passing The Spa Hotel on the right. Turn right into Rusthall Road, following the sign towards High Rocks. After about two hundred yards turn right into a tarmac footpath just beyond a bus stop.*

3. *Proceed downhill through woodland and continue as path leads into a lane, passing Toad Rock on the left, before turning left into Upper Street. At the end of this road take the left-hand footpath and proceed uphill through woods. Continue straight ahead along tarmac path, crossing over two roads (WITH CAUTION) before reaching the church.*

4. *Turn right and follow dirt footpath beside churchyard wall. Turn left and proceed downhill, still flanking churchyard wall on the left. At the bottom of the hill pass through a metal barrier and follow tarmac footpath running beside a lane (The Midway). Proceed past a turning to the left, keeping to footpath as it eventually leads into a farm track (still The Midway). Continue downhill along track to reach a lane.*

5. *Turn left along lane and at the point where the lane swings sharply left into Hungershall Park, go straight ahead into Cabbage Stalk Lane. Continue to end of this lane and cross over a tarmac footpath, then take the right path at a fork opposite (indicated by a No Cycling sign). Proceed through woods to end of this footpath, finally reaching corner of Major York's Road and London Road.*

ACCESS BY BUS AND TRAIN
To Tunbridge Wells from most surrounding areas.

exhaustion (to say nothing of their little legs!) on a natural sandy beach and in a network of flat tops and narrow walkways leading through these famous golden outcrops of sandstone.

To overcome an understandable reluctance on the part of youngsters to leave such paradise, there is an unbeatable incentive: a curious collection of sandstone outcrops at Denny Bottom on Rusthall Common, taking their name collectively from the central rock, known because of its striking likeness, as Toad Rock.

Further exploration to other famous outcrops can be made, including the privately-owned High Rocks, which charges a small entrance fee, and Harrisons Rocks, known also to ardent climbers.

The homeward stretch past the exclusive residences along a quiet lane called The Midway and then through the peaceful Cabbage Stalk Lane back to Tunbridge Wells Common, concludes a marvellous family outing.

Refreshments   At one of many pubs or tearooms in Tunbridge Wells or a picnic on the route.

GEESE AT MARTIN'S FARM

Route 4   7 miles
Frant

Outline Frant ~ Eridge Old Park ~ Eridge Green ~ Whitehill Wood ~ Frant.

Summary From the tiny, peaceful village of Frant, where fragments of pottery have been found which suggest human habitation since 100 B.C., this walk crosses over and leaves behind the busy A267 and descends sharply through woods into the undulating open spaces of Eridge Old Park. Passing beneath a massive beech tree, the route enters more woods, running alongside a stream and beside a large pond (ideal for a picnic!), before crossing a huge field with breathtaking views in all directions, including Eridge Park towards the right. From the small, but picturesque Eridge Green the route then includes a stretch along the busy A26 (where children should be closely supervised), before returning to Frant along a beautiful, winding path through Whitehill Wood. In late Spring and early Summer this part of the walk is a riot of colour with flowering rhododendrons.

Attractions As a bumble-bee blunders along Frant High Street on a sunny day and a visitor lingers to enjoy the delightful setting of the Church of St. Alban, the soothing tinkle of a piano may be heard floating on the breeze, coming from a charming nearby cottage. Yet it wasn't always so tranquil. During the late 16th Century and early 17th Century the village resounded with the noise of the furnaces and water-driven forge-hammers in Eridge Park, the practice finally ceasing because of a shortage of timber.

   Along the route leading down from the A267 there are lovely glimpses through the trees across the valley below, while the flat, grassy path through a section of Eridge Old Park at the bottom of the hill will have children running up and down with glee. The entrance to more woods is gradually marked by a gathering of enormous beeches and lovely, pink-tinged Scots pines standing by the bank of a stream. Very early in Spring the yellow brimstone butterfly can be seen here, its caterpillars having fed on buckthorn. Later come the small tortoiseshell butterflies, their caterpillars nourished on stinging nettles and then come the orange tips, the food of their caterpillars being the unmistakable garlic mustard.

   In August visitors may suddenly be surprised, as they pick their way down the steep slope through woodland near the start of the walk, by a mass of Indian balsam flowers, their stems so tall and their blossoms so

continued on page 22

19

Route 4

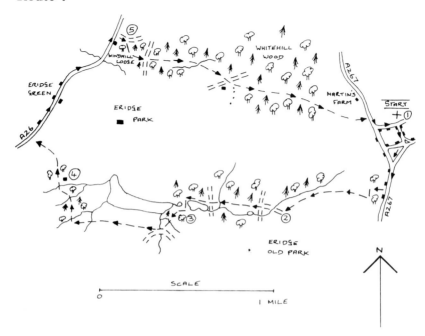

SCALE

0   1 MILE

FRANT HIGH STREET

Route 4
Frant

7 miles

START *at the church (corner of High Street and Church Lane) (O.S. Pathfinder 1248 G.R.590356), approached by A267. Park near church.*

ROUTE

1. *From church walk straight down High Street passing The George on the left and keeping to the right at a fork in the road. As High Street swings sharply left, cross over the intersecting road ahead and follow footpath across the green. On reaching A267 turn left. After about a hundred and fifty yards (just past Thornbury on the right) cross over the A267 and follow a footpath between two fences. Continue downhill through woods, turning left along a track at the bottom for several yards before turning right and proceeding straight ahead along a grassy path through an open space. Pass through a kissing gate into woods. Follow a long, winding path along left-hand fringe of woods.*

2. *Turn right into a track near a metal gate (indicated by a yellow arrow) and after about twenty yards cross a stream via a concrete bridge. Follow track uphill through woods. Cross over an intersecting track and follow indicated footpath. Continue along path, crossing a bridge made of chopped logs. Continue straight across an intersection of tracks, eventually turning left along the bank of a large pond (WITH CAUTION).*

3. *Turn right at the end of the bank, taking indicated path along fringe of woods. Cross a small bridge and after a further fifty yards continue as path leads into a track. Cross an earthen bridge, bearing right immediately afterwards to pass through a kissing gate. Bearing slightly right again follow indicated path through a large field. Cross a footbridge and after about twenty yards turn right into woods along indicated path, crossing a second bridge shortly afterwards. Continue through woods, cross another bridge and then bear left along indicated path. After twenty yards turn right, crossing another bridge straight ahead.*

4. *Proceed uphill along right border of a field. Continue in direction of footpath sign through a small band of woods. Cross a stile and follow right border of another field (ignoring a kissing gate on the right). Continue along right border (as it bears gently downhill to the left) and pass through a gateway indicated by a yellow arrow. Proceed along right border of another field. Pass through a kissing gate and turn right (WITH CAUTION) into A26, continuing for about three quarters of a mile before turning right into a track just beyond Windmill Lodge.*

5. *After about a hundred yards (as track bears left) turn right along indicated footpath into woods. After several hundred yards cross over an intersecting track, taking indicated footpath facing you. Follow long winding path through woods, crossing over a log bridge before eventually crossing over another intersecting track (beside a house). Take indicated path facing you and after a short distance fork left. Continue along path straight ahead all the way to its end. Cross a stile (slightly to the left) and walk along the right-hand boundary of a field, crossing a second stile and passing through a second field, again along the right-hand boundary. Cross a third stile and then after about five yards (WITH EXTREME CAUTION) pass through a kissing gate and cross over the A267. Turn right and after about a hundred yards turn left into Church Lane to reach the High Street.*

ACCESS BY BUS
To Frant from Heathfield and Tunbridge Wells.

---

thick that they may seem for a moment like a floating pink carpet! Also at this time of year parts of the route through the woods are bordered with a profusion of rosebay willow herb, their pods splitting to release soft fluffy strands like cotton wool, packed full of seeds. Patches of purple heather also make a lovely sight along the way. Look out too for the tiny, yellow tormentil, a four-petalled flower which first comes out in May.

Children may spot a rabbit or a yellow-breasted bluetit and if they are very quiet, and unless it sees them first, they may even see an adder slithering away into the undergrowth towards the water. They might also see one of its favourite meals, a little frog waiting patiently (as if minding its own business) for a juicy insect as it noses innocently through the reeds. Adults may ponder on the beautiful, yet serious business of nature, while youngsters may simply be prompted by a sighting to have a quick game of leap-frog at a suitably flat section of the walk.

With so many springs, streams and ponds in the vicinity, the refreshing sound of running water can often be heard mingling pleasantly with birdsong and, in the sunshine, through the foliage of the trees, an occasional flash of silver can be seen beside a grassy verge. Take note, however, that after rains the area becomes very muddy.

Towards the end of the walk both young and old may enjoy the sight of waddling geese at Martin's Farm, although the birds shouldn't be interfered with (in case they get too Frant-ic!).

Refreshments   At the George or the Abergavenny Arms in Frant, or the Nevill Crest and Gun in Eridge Green.

Route 5 4 miles
Rotherfield

Outline   Rotherfield ~ Rotherhurst Farm ~ Lews Farm ~ Horsegrove Farm ~ Rotherfield.

Summary   The cooling shade of well-established oaks and a wide hillside avenue, which overlooks the sweeping green lawns of a golfcourse and the undulating, neatly-divided farmland beyond, will prove very refreshing on a hot, sunny day, as well as being an added incentive to continue the adventure. The route continues past the old oast of Rotherhurst Farm and then a row of lovely cottages and gardens along a busy, but brief stretch of the B2101, before passing along Sheriff's Lane, with its breathtaking views in all directions, including the well-known local landmark, the shingled spire of the Church of St. Denys in Rotherfield. Since the ground in many places is uneven and some of the stiles are high, this should be described as a rather demanding walk, although the rewards are so rich that some adventurers may find themselves back in Rotherfield all too soon. Exploration of this quaint Sussex village, however, should provide plenty of further enjoyment.

Attractions   With far-reaching views over the rolling Wealden hills a visitor to this beautiful area may feel on top of the world. In striking contrast, though, they could suddenly feel quite dwarfed on turning into a lane near Rotherhurst, where the air is sometimes split in Spring with the cawing of rooks circling high above, as they protect their lofty nests in the branches of gigantic Scots pines, a sight that could, with a gentle nudge of the imagination, belong to the world of myths or the supernatural.

The family may perhaps share a chuckle too, on the subject of myths, since according to local folklore the ladies of Rotherfield were known for their unusually long legs, the puzzle being whether this was caused by an additional pair of ribs or because they had to be dragged out so often from the exceptionally sticky clay in the region! Beware, after rain certain parts of the route may, along with steadily growing mounds of clay on even the most circumspect of shoes, tend to tip the scales in favour of the latter!

Passing up hill and down dale, this walk is peppered with a fascinating variety of environments. Children can play safely in several wide open spaces and they are bound to enjoy seeing the many farm animals along the way, a notable spot being towards the end of the route where two steeply sloping fields meet in a hedgerowed hollow through which flows a little stream. On one slope a cow may pause from grazing to

continued on page 26

Route 5

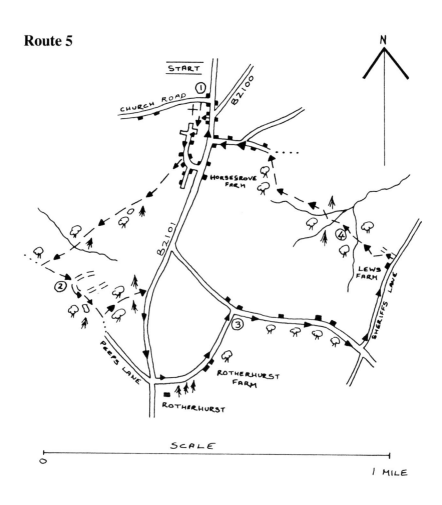

SCALE

0   1 MILE

VIOLET (blue March - April)

Route 5

Rotherfield

4 miles

START   *in Church Road (B2100) (O.S. Pathfinder 1269 G.R.557298), approached by A26 or A267. Park in Church Road.*

ROUTE

1. *From Church Road (beside The George) pass through a kissing gate and take path through churchyard, leaving through another kissing gate. Proceed straight ahead through a private car park and along pathway between houses. Turn right into a lane and then left. As lane swings sharply left, continue straight ahead along pathway between houses. Pass through another kissing gate and follow path between hedges (be careful of footing as the ground here is very uneven!). Proceed straight ahead through a gateway and follow track leading past a pond on the left and then straight ahead into a field. About halfway through field bear slightly left before crossing a bridge with a stile at either end. Bearing slightly right, proceed uphill through golf course. At the top of the hill turn left along indicated bridleway.*

2. *After about a hundred yards turn right at a T-junction and follow track as it swings immediately to the left. On reaching an intersection, continue uphill along indicated footpath. Pass through gate, turn left and cross over a stile. Follow path to a lane. Turn right and continue (WITH CAUTION), over brow of hill. After about another two hundred yards turn left into another lane (opposite Peeps Lane). Continue to end of lane.*

3. *At a T-junction, turn right (WITH CAUTION) and, after several hundred yards, turn left into Sheriff's Lane. Just beyond Lews Farm, turn left through gateway into track and after about twenty yards cross a stile on the left into a field. Continue straight ahead, crossing another stile (or passing through gateway). Follow righthand boundary of another field before leaving it via a stile in the corner. Follow path downhill and cross a bridge before climbing over a fortified section of a fence.*

4. *Bearing right, cross a field, then a stile into another field. Follow right-hand boundary, continuing straight into a small band of woods before crossing another stile. Cross stream via stone steps, then a wooden bridge over another stream, immediately followed by a stile. Proceed diagonally towards the left across a field, eventually leaving via a stile in the top corner. Continue along left-hand boundary of another field, leaving it via a stile in the corner. Proceed along a lane, continuing*

as it leads into a road. Follow road uphill and then turn right along High Street. Just past The Rotherfield Village Antiques (opposite the King's Arms), turn left into a lane leading to churchyard. Retrace steps to car.

ACCESS BY BUS
To Rotherfield from Crowborough, Heathfield and Tunbridge Wells.

---

let a calf suckle at her side, while on the other slope sheep might catch the eye of their observers as little lambs gambol innocently on the grass.

Also full of youthful energy, children will not hesitate when presented with tempting wooden bridges, gates, stiles and a fortified section of fencing to scale, while straggling parents might take a breather, using the perfectly legitimate excuse of wishing to savour one of the views or to linger in awe on the bank of a stream dotted in Spring with yellow lesser celandine, white wood anemones, primroses and lilac cuckoo flowers.

Refreshments   At the King's Arms, The George, The Catts Inn or perhaps Mansion House Tea Rooms in Rotherfield.

MAYFIELD FRIENDS

Route 6   3½ miles

Mayfield

Outline Mayfield ~ Luckhurst Crouch Farm ~ Vicarage Wood ~ Glebe Farm ~ The Old Palace (now St. Leonard's Mayfield School) ~ Mayfield.

Summary If anyone can refrain from an occasional forgetful daydream, they might perhaps be able to disprove a suggestion that this ramble through the High Weald of East Sussex may be a walk of a thousand views. The sheer magnitude of the constantly expanding and altering outlooks should not only rule out the very possibility of keeping count, but will probably leave the visitor pleasantly stunned. For those already stunned after simply reading the route description, which might invoke thoughts of a gruelling mountain assault course, an incentive may be a refreshing drink on completion of the walk in the idyllic setting of the garden behind the 16th Century Middle House Hotel. Adults can look back with pride and pleasure over the beautiful Wealden hills, which they will have personally traversed, while children can play on a nearby climbing frame. Should they have the energy, of course, after a route so full of grassy slopes, challenging stiles, steps, gates, footbridges and fences to scale that even the wildest young lust for adventure should be fully satisfied.

Attractions Mayfield derives its name from the Old English word Maghfeld, meaning Maid's Field. The colourful village sign portrays a maid with children at play, while beneath them the heroic St. Dunstan, Archbishop of Canterbury from 960 to 988, soundly clamps the Devil's nose with a pair of red-hot tongs. According to local folklore the Devil then leapt in agony into a spring near Tunbridge Wells, the reason for the water's distinctive taste. The famous tongs were preserved in the convent, now St. Leonard's Mayfield School, which was originally Mayfield Palace and was used by the archbishops for over two centuries before being given to King Henry VIII.

While the Devil must surely know exactly what he'd be in for if he ever set foot again in this otherwise friendly village, today's visitors, who may be reluctant to start the walk and forego the immediate prospect of exploring the fascinating High Street, can at least feel confident that a warm welcome will still prevail on their return. Tea at three might be just the answer in the quaint April Cottage, next to May Cottage, beside of course June Cottage, all in a pretty row in nearby West Street.

continued on page 30

Route 6

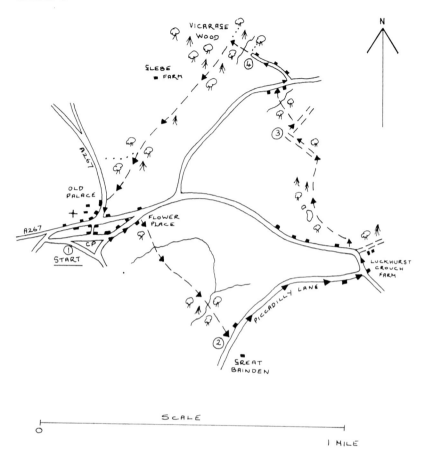

VICARAGE WOOD

GLEBE FARM

④

③

A267

OLD PALACE

A267

FLOWER PLACE

CP

① START

②

PICCADILLY LANE

LUCKHURST CROUCH FARM

GREAT BAINDEN

N

SCALE

0

1 MILE

Route 6

Mayfield   3½ miles

START *at the car park in South Street (O.S. Pathfinder 1269 G.R.587269), approached from Star Lane off High Street (A267).*

ROUTE

1. *Turn right from car park into The Avenue, continuing almost to its end. Just beyond Flower Place, turn right into footpath, continuing downhill and over a stile. Proceed along right-hand boundary of a field, bearing left just before reaching the corner and then right after about fifty yards to pass over a grassy bridge. Continue uphill through a second field. Cross a fortified section of fencing in top left corner, continuing through third field and through a gap in a hedge. Proceed downhill along right-hand boundary of fourth field. Cross a stile, descend steps into woods and cross a footbridge, before proceeding uphill and over a stile. Continue uphill along left-hand boundary of two fields, scaling another stile between them.*

2. *Cross a stile and then turn left, following a lane to its end. Turn left at a T-junction (towards Mayfield) and follow another lane uphill as it swings to the left. Just past the driveways to The Mill House and Merrieweather Cottages, turn right and cross a stile. Turn left and follow long left-hand boundary of two fields, crossing a stile (beside a gateway) between them. Cross another stile and, bearing slightly right, cross a third field. Pass through a gateway halfway down the opposite boundary. Follow a track along right-hand boundary of fourth field.*

3. *Cross a stile in right-hand corner and after about twenty yards cross another stile on the left. Bearing slightly right, cross through a field. Climb down a sloping ladder between two trees, before passing through a gate, shortly followed by a small footbridge! Proceed uphill along right-hand boundary of two fields, crossing two further stiles. Turn right and proceed along a driveway, turning right into a lane. After about twenty yards turn left, proceeding to the end of another lane (marked private, but also indicated by stone sign as public footpath).*

4. *Continue straight ahead along a path through woods, crossing a footbridge before eventually turning left at a T-junction of paths. Continue along path and pass under a wooden barrier. Keeping to left-hand boundaries, proceed uphill through four fields, crossing three stiles. Cross a fourth stile and, bearing slightly left, ascend small slope, following right-hand boundary of two playing fields. Continue through car park of Memorial Hall and turn left into a lane (A267). Follow lane*

as it swings sharply right into High Street and after about twenty yards turn left into Star Lane, leading back to car park.

ACCESS BY BUS
To Mayfield from Tunbridge Wells, Crowborough and Heathfield.

Passing through so much farmland, the route will provide constant sightings of horses, cattle and sheep grazing on steeply sloping fields, which are divided by lovely trees and hedgerows. It is worth looking back regularly while climbing the long slope to Piccadilly Lane to appreciate the rapidly extending views including the village on top of the opposite hill, with the spire of St. Dunstan's Church in the middle. Along the lane a little stealth may reveal a robin, great tit, pied wagtail or chaffinch before it flits away out of a tree or from a clump of blackthorn, hawthorn, coppiced ash or holly.

On crossing a stile near the entrance to Merrieweather Cottages, the family will be further enthralled by yet another panoramic sweep across the rolling Sussex hills and on the edge of a wide, grassy field where children can dash about quite safely, this could be the perfect spot for a picnic.

For youngsters the best could yet be to come: stepping between two enormous oaks, the intrepid explorer must descend a steeply sloping ladder, pass through a gate and then, perhaps after a friendly greeting from a horse or benevolent donkey, continue over a little bridge through boggy ground and uphill over two more stiles!

Remember to look back regularly from the path leading uphill past the double oasts of Glebe Farm to enjoy even more magnificent views into the bountiful heart of the Weald.

Refreshments   At the Carpenters Arms, the Middle House Hotel or tea at April Cottage in West Street (served at 3.00 p.m.).

Burwash

Outline   Burwash ~ Bateman's ~ Bog Wood ~ Burnt House Farm ~
Rye Green Farm ~ Bateman's ~ Burwash.

Summary   Perhaps with imaginations stimulated after a recent reading
of one of Rudyard Kipling's poems or stories, children can clamber
energetically over stiles and rush through farmland along wide, grassy
paths on the way to Bateman's, the author's former home, while adults
should surely be forgiven if they find it hard to keep their own heads
entirely, when confronted by the view downhill along a line of inviting,
well-established oaks into the splendid valley of the River Dudwell. A
lovely contrast to this impressive openness is provided on entering Bog
Wood, a beautiful and peaceful world all of its own, where the sound of
shallow, tinkling water complements the soothing, if not restrained,
orchestra of birdsong. Sheep and sometimes lambs can be seen in the
fields of Burnt House Farm as more views unfold, first to the right
towards Park Wood, then over the valley to the left with the spire of
Burwash church visible in the distance and then, to crown it all, a
bird's-eye view of Bateman's and the length of the valley beyond.

Attractions   During the 18th and early 19th Century, simply living in a
village like Burwash probably meant being involved with the thriving
business of smuggling. After the decline of the iron industry there wasn't
much else to do for a living and unemployment was high. In from the
Continent came spirits, perfume, lace and tea, which were then hidden in
houses specially built for the purpose! With a fortune being lost in duty
and with most pipes packed with smuggled tobacco, the Government
finally curbed this illegal trade around 1830 by introducing the
Coastguard Service and the village policeman.

Providing evidence of the earlier prosperity of the iron industry, and
now owned by the National Trust, is the 17th Century Bateman's, home
of Rudyard Kipling between 1902 and 1936. Visitors can see the study
where some of his wonderful stories were written. Set in the valley of the
River Dudwell and embraced by rolling Sussex farmland, there are also
lovely gardens to explore, with conveniently placed benches, including a
picturesque path to a restored 18th Century watermill, adapted by
Kipling in 1903 to provide electricity for the house.

Young and old alike will enjoy walking around the edge of the mill
pond and across a little wooden bridge before strolling along a grassy

continued on page 34

C   31

Route 7

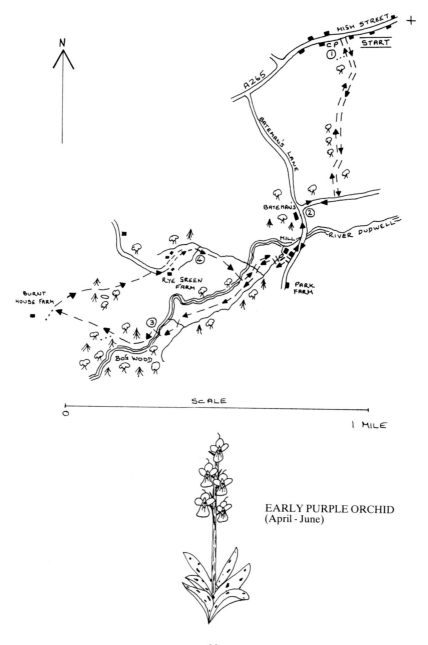

N

HISH STREET

START

CP

A265

BATEMAN'S LANE

BATEMAN'S

RIVER DUDWELL

MILL

PARK FARM

RYE GREEN FARM

BURNT HOUSE FARM

BOG WOOD

SCALE

0

1 MILE

EARLY PURPLE ORCHID
(April - June)

32

Route 7

Burwash

START *from car park in High Street (beside The Bear Hotel) (O.S. Pathfinder 1270 G.R.674247), approached by A265.*

ROUTE

1. *Take path from rear left-hand corner of car park. Cross stile and continue downhill along a right-hand boundary of a field. Turn right over bridge, immediately followed by stile. Proceed along path through second field. Cross another stile and continue along right-hand boundary of third field, crossing a stile to the right. Cross diagonally to the left through fourth field, leaving it via another stile in far right-hand corner. Continue downhill along left-hand boundary of fifth field. Cross stile and turn right along a lane.*

2. *On reaching a T-junction (in front of Bateman's) turn left into lane towards Park Farm. Continue over bridge and just beyond Corner Cottage turn right into track. Turn left along path just before mill pond, turning right over bridge and then left along a grassy bank. Proceed as path bears left, passing over a bridge. Continue along winding path (ignoring a bridge on the right), eventually crossing a stile. Proceed first through the centre of one field and then along the left-hand boundary of a second. Pass through a gateway and over a bridge in the far left corner of the field, bearing slightly right along a path through another field.*

3. *After about a hundred yards turn right through a gateway and over a bridge. Turn immediately left, following path beside river and up a steep slope before crossing a stile on the left. Continue uphill through woods, eventually crossing a stile on the right. Proceed uphill along right boundary of a field towards Burnt House Farm. On reaching the top right corner of the field turn sharp right through a gate and continue along left boundary of another field. Pass through another gate and proceed straight ahead through another field. Cross a stile, follow path through trees. Cross through a field, bearing slightly towards the right (in the direction of Bateman's), and pass through an opening in the hedgerow facing you (far right corner of field). Turn right into a lane, bearing left almost immediately as it leads into a track (just past Rye Green Farm). Continue downhill, cross a stile and continue along right boundary of a field.*

4. *Cross a stile to the right, immediately followed by a bridge and turn left along boundary of another field. After about a hundred yards bear slightly right, crossing through the field. Cross a bridge and turn left into grassy path through woods. From this point you retrace your steps over the earlier part of walk, leading past the mill pond and Bateman's, along a lane and then up through five fields to car park.*

---

bank beside the millstream, which is lined on the opposite bank with alders, their branches leaning out over the water. Throughout the year the rich green grass in the fields may be speckled with the striking blue and white flowers of the common field speedwell, while in the woods during Spring, as well as a mass of bluebells, lesser celandine, wood anemones and greater stitchwort, a lucky visitor may see the remarkable spotted leaves and delicate flowers of the early purple orchid. Sharing an appreciation of the flora, an orange-tipped butterfly may settle to feed on the nectar of a lilac cuckoo flower. Between June and August, particularly attractive in a splash of sunshine, rich clusters of purple loosestrife may be an absorbing and relaxing sight, as bees and butterflies busy themselves about their flowers, no wonder perhaps that the plant was apparently used in the old days to soothe a quarrel!

For bird-lovers who may already have spotted a bluetit, robin, chaffinch or housemartin near the mill, a further pleasure might be the sight of a tiny, black-capped willow tit, gathering material for a nest, still managing a chirp even with its beak full of grass!

Refreshments   At Kipling's Bar, The Bell Inn or the Chaunt House Tea Rooms.

BEWL RESERVOIR

Route 8   4½ miles
Wadhurst and Bewl Bridge Reservoir

Outline   Wadhurst ~ Little Pell Farm ~ Bewl Bridge Reservoir ~ Little Whiligh ~ Long Wood ~ Wadhurst.

Summary   In the early days, dating back to Roman times, iron was mined around the charming village of Wadhurst although today the land is agricultural, largely devoted to sheep-farming. This will provide an endless source of pleasure for children who may well wonder just what their animal friends are thinking as they lift their heads from the rich pasture to stare back through fences and hedgerows at their observers with something very similar to human curiosity. Adults are bound to enjoy the many sweeping views over delightful undulating fields, dotted with clumps of well-established woodland, magnificent oast houses and lovely cottages, to say nothing of the impressive outlook over Bewl Bridge Reservoir, an area teeming with bird life. From various points along the route the distinctive spire of Wadhurst church is clearly visible, providing both a beautiful sight and also a handy reference.

Attractions   A good pair of binoculars may be an asset on this route which includes part of the Bewl Bridge Reservoir. Both parents and children can share the excitement of picking out and trying to identify a staggering variety of birds in the area, part of which has been set aside as a nature conservation site managed by the Sussex Trust for Nature Conservation. Permanent residents of the reservoir include mallards, moorhens, coots and the great crested grebe, while migrant birds such as warblers, whinchats or tern sometimes stop over for a rest on their long flights. Late in the Summer other visitors arrive, such as wagtails, reed-bunting and willow warblers. The elegant posture of a grey heron, as it waits poised for a snack of frogs or fish, is certainly memorable.

More detailed information about Bewl, including a calendar of special events, is available from the Visitors' Centre on the north bank (approached from the A21 near Lamberhurst), adjacent to which is an adventure playground and wooden arc for children.

In the woods the family can listen for the hammering of the green woodpecker or keep a look out for the fascinating antics of the speedy nuthatch (usually found where there are oaks), as well as blackbirds hopping in and out of ferns or cautious robins looking down and whistling from lofty branches. Less dense areas of woodland are full of wildflowers at their respective times of year, such as bluebells, foxgloves and campions.

continued on page 38

35

Route 8

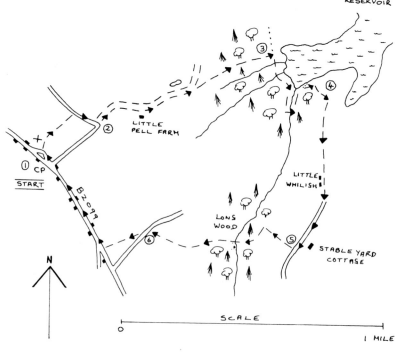

BEWL BRIDGE RESERVOIR

LITTLE PELL FARM

② ③ ④

① CP

START

B2099

LITTLE WHILISH

LONS WOOD

⑤ STABLE YARD COTTAGE

⑥

N

SCALE

0   1 MILE

HERON (grey and white 90cm)

Route 8

Wadhurst and Bewl Bridge Reservoir   4½ miles

START *from the car park off the High Street (B2099) in Wadhurst behind the Greyhound public house (O.S. Pathfinder 1249 G.R.640318), approached by A267.*

ROUTE

1. *Leave car park and cross over High Street, turning left into street behind National Westminster Bank. Continue to end of street, before taking right-hand path through churchyard. Just beyond the church, turn right through a kissing gate and follow a footpath, before eventually turning right into a lane. Follow lane downhill.*

2. *At the bottom of the hill, where lane swings to the right, turn left into a dirt track, passing through the gates of Little Pell Farm. Ignore a turning on the left to Little Pell Barn and continue straight on through farmyard. Cross a stile and follow a track. Cross a second stile and continue downhill along track. At a point where track bears left to meet two adjacent farm gates, continue straight ahead along a grassy path which leads into woodland.*

3. *After crossing two stiles, turn right at a T-junction. Follow path over a hill and cross a stream (which passes through a pipe beneath) and then cross another stream via a wooden bridge. Continue along path as it bears right, eventually crossing a second wooden bridge (CAUTION: STEEP DROPS). Follow path uphill as it swings left and then right, keeping right at a fork.*

4. *As path leaves the woods, cross a stile to the right and cross diagonally towards the left through a field. Continue along irregular right-hand boundary, eventually passing through a wooden gate. Follow left edge of a second field and pass through another gate. Continue along path which eventually leads through another gate into farmyard of Little Whiligh. Keep straight ahead, passing through two further gates before following a concrete road up a hill.*

5. *Just past Stable Yard Cottage, turn right (indicated by yellow arrow), descending a flight of steps through a kissing gate into a field. Continue downhill along right edge of field. At the bottom of the hill turn left along a path through Long Wood, eventually bearing right to pass through a wooden gate and cross over a bridge. Follow a path up a long, steep hill along the left edge of a field.*

6. *Cross a stile at the top of the hill and then cross a lane before crossing a second stile into another field. Cross this field diagonally to the left. Cross a stile and turn right into High Street (WITH CAUTION), continuing to town centre and car park.*

ACCESS BY BUS
To Wadhurst from Turnbridge Wells and Hawkhurst.

Fertilizers and weedkillers are not favoured in the grasslands around Bewl which means there has been a steady increase in plant life, including clovers, vetches and ox-eyed daisies. A variety of butterflies can also be seen on sunny days and, with a more sinister intent, yet just as beautiful, an occasional kestrel may be spotted hovering as it looks for mice or voles in the fields.

Refreshments At the Greyhound or the White Hart public houses, a cosy nook called The Cottage Tea Room or perhaps a picnic on the walk.

DOWN FARM OAST

38

Route 9 **3½ miles**

Lamberhurst

Outline   Lamberhurst ~ Scotney Castle Estate ~ Woodland Walk ~ Lamberhurst Vineyards (Ridge Farm) ~ Lamberhurst.

Summary   The gently rolling hills around the village of Lamberhurst provide the walker with easy access to a delightful range of far-reaching views. On a neighbouring hill, from one of the first vantage points, St. Mary's Church can be seen, with the imposing walls of Court Lodge next to it, while looking back across the Teise valley towards Lamberhurst there is an interesting patchwork of farmland, with the well-kept fairways and greens of the golf course and the neat playing fields beside the High Street, itself backed by rising hills. Early in the walk the distinctive line of the four oasts making up Down Farm Oast can be seen towards the right in the distance and children can look forward to a close-up view later as the route goes right past them. The view of the village from the heights of the vineyards is also unforgettable.

Attractions   Radiating out from the central jewel of Lamberhurst is a scintillating array of other attractions, including Owl House, home of the 'owlers' or smugglers in the 18th Century, its surrounds now a legitimate treasure for garden-lovers; The Toy and Model Museum with an entertaining model display; Finchcocks, built in 1725, now a museum of keyboard instruments, also offering music recitals; Scotney Castle, a moated 14th Century defence against the French, known for its lovely gardens and idyllic setting; Bewl Water with a waterside walk, picnic areas and water sports and of course the beautiful Lamberhurst Vineyards at Ridge Farm, one of the largest vineyards in Britain!

Once the centre of the iron industry in the Weald, Lamberhurst is known for the railings at St. Paul's Cathedral, which were made at Gloucester Forge, named after Queen Anne's son, the Duke of Gloucester. The village is divided by the River Teise, which used to be the county border between Kent and Sussex. The higher price offered for hops in the county made the villagers decide in 1894 that they should be wholly part of Kent. The two pubs on either side of the Teise, the Chequers and the George and Dragon, were used by stranded travellers in times of flooding.

Scotney Castle Gardens are easily reached from the route and make a very pleasant diversion. The magnificent gardens were created in the quarry that supplied the stone for the overlooking manor house, which

continued on page 42

39

Route 9

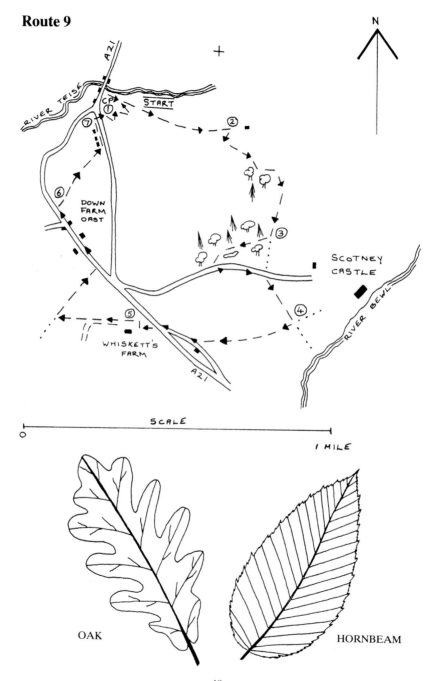

N

RIVER TEISE

A21

CP

START

① ⑦

② ■

③

SCOTNEY
CASTLE

RIVER BEWL

⑥

DOWN
FARM
OAST

④

⑤

WHISKETT'S
FARM

A21

SCALE

0   1 MILE

OAK

HORNBEAM

Route 9

Lamberhurst   3½ miles

START   *at car park next to The Chequers in the High Street (O.S. Pathfinder 1249 G.R.677362), off the A21.*

ROUTE

1. *Leave car park through back gate and cross two playing fields. Cross a stile in the far right corner of second field and follow a footpath across a golf course fairway. Cross a wooden barrier and continue in the direction of a yellow arrow over a second fairway. Cross a stile directly ahead and then cross over a strip of farmland to reach a concrete track, following it straight up a hill.*

2. *At the top of the track cross a stile to the right and proceed along the left boundary of a field. Cross another stile marked Scotney Castle Estate and, after a short distance, turn left through a forked gap in the fence. Turn right, following the irregular boundary of another field in the direction of yellow arrows.*

3. *Cross a stile and bear slightly right, proceeding uphill in the direction of a green arrow indicating the Woodland Walk. Continue through woods, eventually turning left into a tarmac lane. After several hundred yards turn right into a field through a gate indicated by a footpath sign to Kilndown. Bearing slightly left, proceed downhill through a field.*

4. *Just before a stone bridge, turn right and follow a grassy track, passing through a gate and then across another field. Pass through a second gate and turn right into a lane. On meeting the A21, cross over (WITH CAUTION), following a public footpath sign into a field directly opposite. Follow right-hand boundary for a hundred yards before turning right through a gap in the hedge into another field.*

5. *Turn left, following boundary of this field and cross driveway of Whiskett's Farm into another field. Follow a track along the left-hand boundary and, as it bears left, take the footpath straight ahead through the field. Cross over a wire fence (using wooden struts supplied for the purpose!) and turn right. Follow a footpath to a lane, turn left and proceed uphill and, as the lane swings left, continue straight into Sand Road.*

6. *After a hundred yards turn right, following the length of a concrete track in the direction of a footpath sign. Bearing slightly right, continue downhill through vineyards along a grassy path between fences. Cross a stile and another field, bearing slightly left. Pass through a gate and*

continue straight down a grassy slope, bearing left along a tarmac footpath to meet the A21.

7. *Cross A21 (WITH CAUTION) and turn left, turning right after ten yards into a driveway indicated by a footpath sign. After twenty yards cross a stile and continue along a gravel track. After another twenty yards turn left into another gravel track which leads into the playing fields adjacent to the car park.*

ACCESS BY BUS

To Lamberhurst from Tunbridge Wells and most surrounding areas.

---

was built in 1837 by the lord of the manor, Richard Hussey. Earlier manor houses were sited in the castle ruins and history recalls a secret priest chamber, which in 1598 saved the life of the Jesuit John Blount.

Much of the route is through farmland and children will enjoy seeing horses or cattle and sheep grazing in the fields. Two benches beside the pond on the route through the peaceful Woodland Walk make a lovely picnic site, while the Brown Trout public house, opposite the mighty building of Down Farm Oast, is an ideal resting point, catering especially for families, with swings and trampolines for children in the garden.

Refreshments   The Brown Trout, The Chequers and The George and Dragon in Lamberhurst, or a picnic on the route.

APPLE BLOSSOM TIME

Route 10

Goudhurst

Outline   Goudhurst ~ Lidwells Lane ~ Trottenden Farm ~ Goudhurst.

Summary   Soon after leaving the village the explorer will be confronted
by an inviting and far-reaching view over the valley of the River Teise.
The white cowls of oasts can be seen dotting the rolling hills, while cattle
and sheep graze peacefully in neatly divided fields. Shortly afterwards a
second panoramic view is unveiled. An entire hillside slope in the
distance may be marked out with the criss-crossed supports for the area's
famous hops and in May the blossom of the orchards may seem like an
artistic splash of pink on the canvas of an impressionist. The route then
descends through the orchards before climbing a gentle slope along the
beautiful Lidwells Lane. A further descent leads to the fields near the
triple oasts of Trottenden Farm, where frisky lambs in Spring may delight
every member of the family. After a further climb there is another chance
to appreciate the view before reaching the village again, perhaps in time
for tea at Weeks of Goudhurst.

Attractions   Although a settlement may have existed there more than a
thousand years ago, Goudhurst only really began to develop after the
invasion of the Normans. Later, in the 14th Century, the cloth trade
brought prosperity to the village when King Edward III arranged for the
immigration of Flemish weavers. In Church Road a row of weavers'
cottages had connecting attics where the cloth was stretched, while other
grand local buildings show evidence of the huge financial rewards of an
enterprise that was to stretch for over four hundred years!

Adding to the wealth, and also the noise, was the iron industry in the
16th Century, when both the forges and the mills involved the use of
heavy hammers which were operated with the water-driven power
harnessed from the many rivers and streams in the area.

When both industries declined in the 18th Century the locals took
advantage of the favourable soil by growing fruit and hops, although
farmers found it difficult to keep labourers who were often lured away by
the much more lucrative business of smuggling, which was rife
throughout the Weald. The ruthless Hawkhurst Gang did not take kindly
to opposition and threatened to burn down the village and slaughter
everyone in it. To their surprise they were ambushed instead and
defeated in the famous Battle of Goudhurst in 1747, by a former army
officer, William Sturt, and a group of brave volunteers.

continued on page 46

43

Route 10

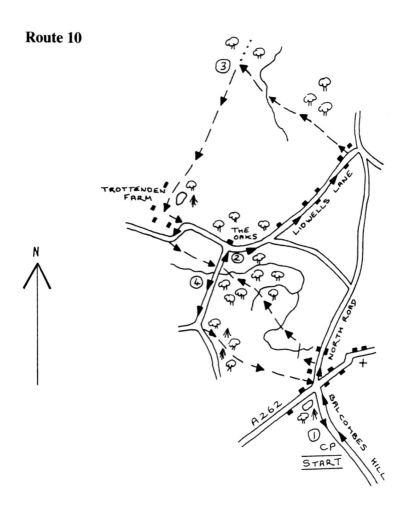

SCALE

0

1 MILE

44

Route 10
Goudhurst

2½ miles

START *at the car park in Balcombes Hill, off the High Street (A262) (O.S. Pathfinder 1249 G.R.722377).*

ROUTE

1. *From car park turn left into Balcombes Hill, continuing past pond and across A262. Proceed down North Road (between The Vine and National Westminster Bank) before turning left along a signposted footpath indicating route to Trottenden Farm. Cross a stile and proceed downhill along right-hand boundary of a field. After about fifty yards cross a second stile and a footbridge on the right. Bearing left, proceed downhill through a field. Cross a third stile and a footbridge, continuing along right-hand boundary of another field. Cross a fourth stile and a footbridge and continue downhill through an orchard. Cross a footbridge and a fifth stile in the corner, before turning right into a lane.*

2. *After about fifty yards turn right into Lidwells Lane. Continue uphill, keeping left at a fork, and just before the end of the lane turn left and proceed down a grassy track in the direction of a stone footpath sign. Cross a stile and continue straight downhill through a field. Cross another stile and continue straight downhill through an orchard. Cross a small earthen bridge and another stile near the far left corner and turn right, following border of a field.*

3. *On reaching a stile in far right-hand corner, turn left, continuing along right-hand border of same field. Cross a stile and proceed through a second field, continuing through a gateway and then along a track. Cross a stile and follow driveway of Trottenden Farm as it swings sharply left. At the end of the driveway turn right into a lane. After about fifty yards cross a stile on the left and pass straight ahead through a field.*

4. *Cross over another stile and turn right, proceeding along another lane. Just after lane swings sharply left, follow an indicated footpath on the left, continuing uphill through woods. Cross a stile and follow the right-hand border of two fields, continuing to the top of a steep hill. Follow a path in the top right corner, cross a stile and continue to the A262. Retrace steps to car park.*

ACCESS BY BUS
To Goudhurst from Tunbridge Wells and Tenterden.

Having enjoyed the views from the hillside which slopes steeply down from the village, and also the openness of the fields near the lovely oasts of Trottenden Farm, the visitor will stroll along a quiet lane, which is flanked by a variety of hedgerows, predominantly hawthorn, with its white May blossom slowly maturing into a lovely pink and then, in September, its deep red haws.

Before returning to Goudhurst, the route then passes through a band of woods, the brightness of bluebells in May lighting up the shade, as striking as the multiple melodies of birdsong in the trees above. Of course managing to actually see those enthusiastic, full-throated performers isn't easy, especially with the thickening foliage of approaching Summer, although an occasional matching of sight and sound will provide the interested observer with a gradually accumulating knowledge which can be extremely satisfying.

Refreshments   At the Vine or the Star and Eagle public houses or Goudhurst Florist and Weeks of Goudhurst Tea Rooms.

CRANBROOK UNION WINDMILL

46

Cranbrook

Outline   Cranbrook ~ Angley Wood ~ Gravel Pit Wood ~ Cranbrook.

Summary   A certain degree of agility may be required for this rewarding, but occasionally rather strenuous route, which leads from the old town of Cranbrook through delightful farmland and fascinating woods, rich with many different kinds of trees, wildflowers and wildlife. While bluebells and rhododendrons offer spectacular splashes of colour in the early part of the year, the area is particularly attractive in Autumn. The soft light of an early October afternoon heightens the lovely contrast between the yellow and green foliage of the many coppiced sweetchestnuts in the woods, while the darker leaves of mighty oaks are tinged with rust, matching the spread of brown through lush carpets of fern beneath. The town itself offers much in the way of refreshments, although some people may prefer a picnic at one of the tables near the children's playground on a hill overlooking the majestic sweeps of the old Union Mill.

Attractions   Situated in the heart of the Kent Weald, and deriving its name from the Crane Brook, the town of Cranbrook became the capital of the woollen industry when Edward III encouraged weavers from Flanders to take up residence and begin business in England, so effectively ending the Flemish monopoly. After the industry's decline the town became the region's agricultural market centre.

The success of the cloth trade is reflected by the magnificence of the church of St. Dunstan, located in true Wealden style at the centre of the town's two main streets, which intersect at right angles. According to legend, an effigy of Father Time descends from the clock tower once a year at midnight to mow the churchyard! Since the money for the clock apparently came from the sale of the parish farm and in the opinion of some parishioners might have been put to better use helping the needy, this may perhaps be seen as an attempt at compensation! The church is also known for the famous Priest's Room above the porch where Sir John Baker, known more commonly as Bloody Baker, kept the Protestants he had so eagerly prosecuted during the reign of Queen Mary.

The mill overlooking the houses of Stone Street is seventy feet high, making it one of the tallest in the country. The fashionable smock-frock of the previous century lends its name to this smock mill, which was built in 1814 and is still in perfect working order. When the original owner,

continued on page 50

Route 11

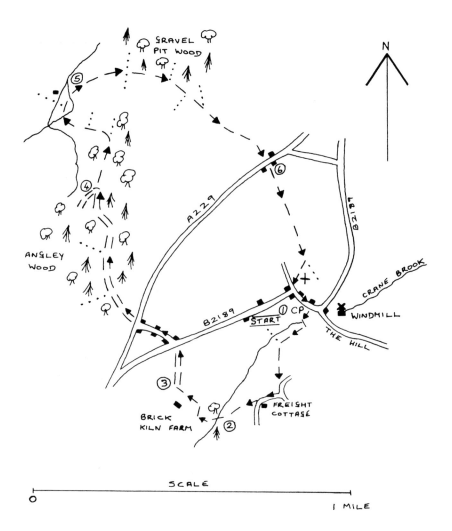

SCALE

O   1 MILE

48

Route 11

Cranbrook   **4 miles**

START   *at the car park (O.S. Pathfinder 1249 G.R.778359) off The Hill near the junction of Stone Street and Waterloo Road (B2189), approached by the A229.*

ROUTE

1. *Take path to the left of Crane Brook (on the left of a dental surgery at the rear of the car park). Proceed past a footpath on the right (to children's playground) and continue as path bears left, eventually leading into Bramley Drive. After ten yards turn right into a lane. Just past Freight Cottage, as lane swings left, continue straight ahead, taking a footpath into woodland.*

2. *Cross a stile and proceed along right-hand boundary of a field for a hundred yards. Cross another stile on the right and follow path into woods. Step across a small stream (Crane Brook) and continue along path before crossing another stile. Proceed uphill and then turn right into a track. Pass through a gateway, cross a field and then another stile. Follow path to the left between fences to reach another track.*

3. *Turn right and continue to the end of the track. Cross a road and follow tarmac footpath directly opposite. Cross over another road and again follow footpath directly opposite (indicated by sign to Glassenbury). Continue straight on, passing a fire warning sign and a main path on the left. At a fork twenty yards further on, take the right-hand path. Continue downhill along main path, as it bends slightly to the left and then to the right.*

4. *At the bottom of the slope, as the main path swings sharply back on itself to the left, take a smaller path to the right. On reaching a fork, take the left-hand path. Proceed downhill, ignoring a path on the right. Continue as path bears right at the bottom of the slope. Cross a stream via a footbridge and after about ten yards, on reaching another fork, take the right-hand path. After another ten yards, cross a second footbridge (children should be very careful of steep drops at both bridges).*

5. *Follow path up a long, steep slope through woods and down the other side, passing stud farm on right. Climb a second slope, passing through an iron kissing gate and then, slightly further on, a wooden one, to reach a driveway. Continue to end of driveway and pass through a gateway.*

6. *Cross over A229 (WITH CAUTION) and take the footpath facing you. After a short distance pass through a kissing gate and then cross over a*

field diagonally towards the right. Pass through another kissing gate and follow path between playing fields, bearing right to reach a lane. Turn left along pavement and pass through another kissing gate, continuing past children's playground before taking the right-hand path through the churchyard. At intersection of Stone Street and the High Street, keep left and continue downhill. Turn right into The Tanyard, which leads back into the car park.

ACCESS BY BUS
To Cranbrook from Tunbridge Wells, Maidstone, Tenterden and Hastings.

———————

Henry Dobell, went bankrupt, the mill passed into the hands of a local partnership, so becoming known as Union Mill.

Having left the town, the early part of the walk may tend to be rather overgrown in places during late Summer, although children will find this an exciting challenge, darting through strips of woodland, clambering over stiles and forging ahead through the narrow walkway between two fences near Brick Kiln Farm. Cattle, sheep and horses can be seen grazing in the farmland, while pheasant and rabbits may be glimpsed in their wilder habitats. Youngsters will also enjoy running up and down the sandy hillocks and in and out of the many tempting little paths in the woods, while adults may enjoy the beautiful picture of purple heather, the exquisite aroma of fern and pine and the perfect moments of peace usually attributed to isolated mountain peaks.

Refreshments   At the George Hotel, The Crown, or a picnic along the route.

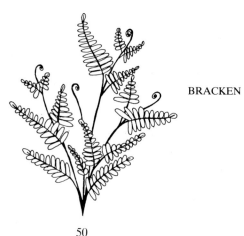

BRACKEN

Route 12

2½ miles

Hawkhurst

Outline   Hawkhurst ~ Rowlands Farm ~ The Moor ~ Hawkhurst.

Summary   Gardens graced with showers of cherry blossom, lilac and, in late May and early June, flaming rhododendrons, as well as many well-established oaks, Scots pines and beech trees, will help to compensate for the noise of traffic along the walkway beside the busy A268 at the start of this short yet most rewarding walk. Peace will prevail on descending North Hill Road, shortly followed by a gentle climb through orchards, a sea of pink and white blossom in May, which will seem like another world altogether. A picnic might be called for on the green of The Moor, the old part of Hawkhurst. Youngsters can play ball or perhaps fly a kite, while parents may be lucky enough to see some real masters of the air, pink-breasted swallows, with their long, forked tails, busily enjoying a picnic of their own, a feast of fresh insects on the wing! The winding trail back to the A268 is splashed with wildflowers in Spring and offers both cooling shade in Summer and also a chance for youngsters in September to replenish empty picnic boxes with juicy blackberries!

Attractions   Having enjoyed four hundred years of prosperity thanks to the woollen industry, which developed after Edward III invited Flemish weavers over from the Continent, Hawkhurst saw the eventual decline of the trade in the 18th Century, coming as a result of the Scottish Act of Union with England, which exposed Kent to severe competition. Like other towns in the area they turned to agriculture, although the notorious smugglers, the Hawkhurst Gang, not only made life difficult for farmers by enticing labourers off the land with the prospect of richer pickings, but also terrorised the entire area, using bribes and threats to avoid prosecution. Those few criminals who were convicted by the reluctant courts were often allowed to escape under discreetly arranged circumstances. The gang was finally defeated in 1747 at the Battle of Goudhurst and although their leader, Tom Kingsmill, managed to escape, he was caught and hung two years later at Tyburn.

Hawkhurst is actually made up of two separate hamlets, Highgate, where the route begins, and the older part called The Moor, each with its own church. Having perhaps enjoyed the odd peep across the valley towards The Moor from the A268, the visitor will soon be able to look back towards Highgate from the beautiful slopes of the orchards, where elegant lines of poplars act as windbreakers and the fields are bordered

continued on page 54

51

Route 12

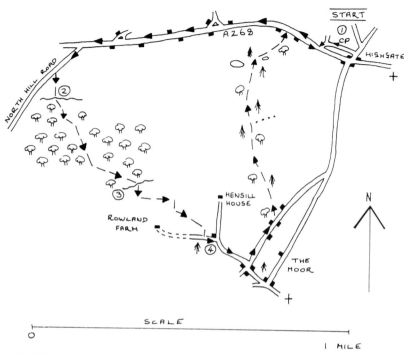

BLUEBELLS

52

Route 12

Hawkhurst
2½ miles

START *from car park in Northgrove Road (O.S. Pathfinder 1249 G.R.760306), off High Street (A268).*

ROUTE

1. *From car park turn right into Northgrove Road and then right into the A268. Continue along right-hand walkway (WITH CAUTION) for about half a mile, passing Hawkhurst village sign on the right. Just past Checker Tree House on the right, turn left into North Hill Road. After about a hundred yards (just past Tackleway on the right) turn left through a gate and proceed downhill in direction of stone footpath sign along left-hand boundary of a field.*

2. *Cross a footbridge and proceed uphill along left-hand boundary of an orchard. After about a hundred yards, cross over a stile on the left and, bearing right, cut across the corner of a field. Cross a stile and continue along left-hand boundary of another orchard. Turn left at the top left corner and proceed along right-hand border of a third orchard.*

3. *Cross stile in far right corner and follow path through woods. Cross another stile and after about fifty yards cross footbridge to the right and then a stile, continuing along right-hand border of a field. Cross a stile, turn left and follow boundary of a second field, turning right in the corner and continuing in same field for about twenty yards before turning left over another stile. Proceed downhill along right-hand boundary of a field for about a hundred yards before turning right down a short path and then left into a lane.*

4. *Follow lane past Hensill House driveway, swinging sharply right and continuing uphill before turning left at a T-junction into Talbot Road. Proceed downhill, passing milk depot on the right and a row of cottages called Mount Pleasant on the left, then turn left into a short driveway. Pass through a kissing gate and follow a winding footpath all the way back up to the A268, ignoring a footpath coming in from the right. Turn right into A268 and retrace steps to car park.*

ACCESS BY BUS
To Hawkhurst from Maidstone and Hastings.

with oaks and variegated hedgerows, including holly and hazel with its clusters of nuts in the Autumn. Bluebells and yellow dandelions in the green grass are a perfect complement to the splendour of the orchard blossom in May, while near the oast of Rowlands Farm, where children might enjoy seeing horses, sheep and cattle, some of the fields may be decked with yellow buttercups and a lavish sprinkling of white daisies.

After passing the Moor Brewery (1841-1924) and the Malt House, and perhaps after a picnic on the village green or a drink in the garden of the Eight Bells Hotel, the explorer will then continue along a fascinating path bordered throughout its length with a continual variety of trees and hedgerows, offering pleasantly surprising views over farmland and, nearer the A268, towards the right, the spire of the church in Highgate.

Refreshments   The Royal Oak in Highgate or the Eight Bells Hotel in The Moor.

BODIAM CASTLE

54

Bodiam Castle

Outline Bodiam Castle ~ Bramley Organic Farm ~ Udiam ~ River Rother ~ Bodiam Castle.

Summary The splendid views across the valley of the River Rother from the beautiful grounds of Bodiam Castle may satisfy many visitors, who will be content to take the airs as they stroll leisurely along the well-appointed gravel walkways, beneath gigantic shady oaks and beside the calm waters of a wide moat, while children romp about on safely sloping lawns, their imaginations tickled by the sight of the impressive castle towers. Others may decide to cross the long wooden bridge to see inside the castle and also further afield from the lofty battlements. There will be those, however, who may also wish to go out and experience that fairy tale landscape at first-hand and this route provides an opportunity to traverse gently rolling hills, pass through rich hedgerowed fields and to delve into pretty, peaceful woods. Further lovely views unfold throughout the route and, having crossed the many stiles, gates, fences and bridges during the earlier part of the walk, the explorer will be able to coast, as if with the river, along a wide, grassy bank all the way back to Bodiam Castle.

Attractions From the raised bank of the River Rother at the start of the walk there is a picture postcard view of the 14th Century Bodiam Castle seated majestically on the hillside slope across the water, while straight ahead is the fitting wealth of beautiful Sussex farmland, fields of which are given over to the bright yellow rapeseed crops, their fragrance during May wafting deliciously through the valley.

Leaving the river, the route leads towards an impressive line of poplars and, on turning once again, the castle can be seen this time to the right, with oast houses now visible on the hillside slopes beyond. More oasts dot the valley ahead, including the triple row at Park Farm, seen more closely towards the left from the river on the final stretch of the walk. Just across the railway tracks, which may yet be revived to extend the Kent and East Sussex Railway, the oasts of Ockham rise behind wooden-fenced paddocks, a delight for all ages in the family.

A long climb follows past willows and oaks and across little streams. Rich red campions may be seen along the way as well as the delicate purple flowers of the common vetch. Lovely views open out from the lane at the top over the valley towards the castle, before the route enters the

continued on page 58

Route 13

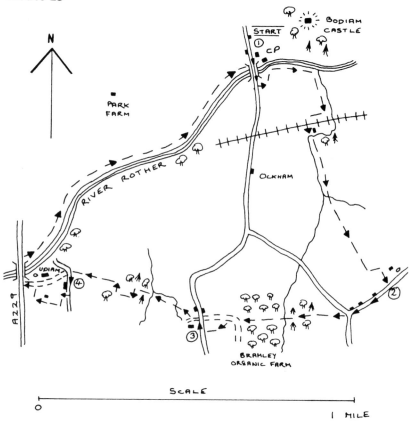

WILLOW TIT (black, white and olive 11cm)

Route 13

Bodiam Castle

4 miles

START   at Bodiam Castle car park (O.S. Pathfinder 1270 G.R.784254), off Bodiam Road, approached by A229.

ROUTE

1. *From car park turn left into Bodiam Road. Cross bridge and turn left through a gateway indicated by footpath sign, bearing left to follow path along raised bank of river. At a gate turn right and proceed along border of a field beside a stream on the left. At far left corner turn right and after about a hundred yards pass through a gate on the left, crossing disused railway line and climbing over a second gate, indicated by yellow arrow. Continue straight ahead, passing a barn on the left before crossing a footbridge. Proceed along right border of a field (keeping to left edge of a boggy patch). Just past a gate on the right, cross another footbridge and a stile in the corner. Follow path up a hill and past a horse chestnut tree, leading roughly parallel to a fence lower down on the left. At the top of the field turn left through a gateway and then right, continuing uphill through an iron gate and along a path between hedges.*

2. *Turn right along a lane and, just past Bodiam turnoff, reach a gate on the right indicated by stone footpath sign. Go through the gate. Proceed diagonally towards the right through a field. Cross a stile in the far right corner and follow path through woods, crossing a footbridge before following signposted path uphill through an orchard. Continue as path leads into a track and after about fifty yards cross a stile on the left. Bearing slightly right, proceed through a field and over another stile (WITH CAUTION).*

3. *Turn right into a lane. After twenty yards turn left into a driveway and then right (signposted footpath), climbing over a gate and continuing downhill along left border of a field. Cross footbridge on the left (CAUTION STEEP DROP), cross stile and continue downhill along right border of a field. Cross another footbridge and another stile, following path into woods. After about twenty yards climb over a stile on the left and then turn right, proceeding uphill along right border of a field. Turn right through a gateway and then left, proceeding downhill along left border of another field before passing through another gate directly ahead.*

4. *Turn left into a lane. Proceed uphill and, just past a row of workshops, turn right into a track and then almost immediately left over a stile. Turn right again and proceed downhill along right border of a field. Cross*

stile on the right, passing through a small field before climbing another stile. Turn left and proceed to the end of a driveway. Pass through gate and (WITH CAUTION) turn right into A229. Just after crossing a bridge turn right, following indicated footpath along bank of river all the way back to Bodiam Castle.

ACCESS BY BUS
To Bodiam from Hastings and Tunbridge Wells.

---

refreshingly different world of woodland, with carpets of bluebells in May beneath the silver birch, hazel, hawthorn, sallow and hornbeam.

Throughout the route children may see the white tails of rabbits disappearing into bushes or bobbing over fields and through the trees, particularly attractive in the orchards of Bramley Organic Farm. Descending towards Udiam, the family will see the well-used dovecotes on the side wall of a stable and, on crossing a stile into a section of the farmyard, where hens may be fussing over little chicks, they will be confronted by a group of magnificent poplars beside a pond, with the buildings of Udiam Farm over to the right, ideally situated beside the meandering River Rother.

Sipping tea perhaps beside the wishing well in the garden of Knolly's next to the castle grounds, while discussing highlights of the walk, including a possible sighting of a skylark hovering over the river with its prolonged, high-pitched cry, the family may feel that their wish for a lovely outing had been truly granted.

Refreshments   The Castle Inn, Knolly's or Bodiam Castle Tea Shop.

COOT (black, white forehead 38cm)

Benenden

Outline   Benenden ~ Benenden School ~ Roman Road ~ Stream Farm ~ Benenden.

Summary   Leaving the tiny, peaceful village of Benenden, one of the oldest settlements in The Weald, this fairly undemanding, yet very satisfying route, leads downhill past the tranquil waters and tree-lined banks of New Pond, before escaping from a rather busy road across a wide, grassy field through a landscape dotted with grazing farm animals, mighty oaks, an occasional copper beech and many huge outcrops of hawthorn, their white blossom in May forming a distinctive feature of the countryside. Charming views unfold as the walk continues through the exclusive grounds of Benenden School, a former pupil there being Princess Anne, who also attended the nearby Moat House Riding School. Along with more beautiful scenery, children and their parents may then enjoy trying to picture life in the days of old as they wander downhill along the course of a Roman road, before turning left at Stream Farm, with its striking double oasts, and then climbing a lengthy, but gentle slope to finally reach a shady lane behind the church. A short stroll downhill past the green brings the visitor back to The Street in Benenden.

Attractions   Benenden began as a pair of Saxon "dens" or clearings in the great, wild forest, where swineherds took their hogs to feed on acorns and oak-masts. When the Romans came they found the forest almost impenetrable, although they did manage to cut a few roads into its depths. At the time of the Domesday Survey in the 11th Century Benenden was one of only four villages in the Weald of Kent to have a church.

Unfortunately the original church was struck by lightning and had to be rebuilt in 1678. It was then restored in 1862 by Lord Cranbrook who also rebuilt the old manor house of Hemsted. Formerly owned by the Guldeford family and visited in 1573 by Queen Elizabeth I, Hemsted was sold to Lord Rothermere and renovated in 1912 before becoming Benenden School. The enormous building, with its tall, slender chimney stacks, can be viewed from several different angles on the walk, each one adding an interesting perspective.

Lovely views open out across the surrounding hills as the route passes through the grounds of the school, where an abundance of well-established trees can be appreciated, including poplar, Scots pine, sweet chestnut, lime, copper beech, hornbeam and that true descendant of the

continued on page 62

Route 14

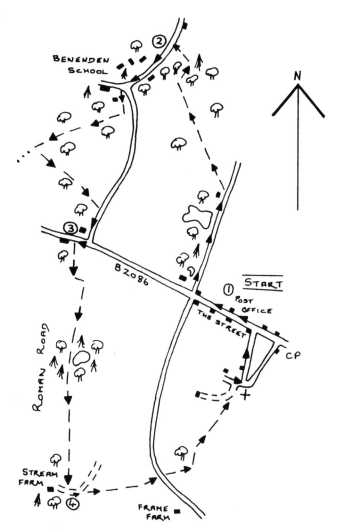

Route 14

Benenden   3 miles

START   *at the Post Office in The Street (B2086) (O.S. Pathfinder 1250 G.R.807329), approached by A229 or A28. Parking in car park beside village hall.*

ROUTE

1. *From Post Office turn right along The Street, turning right again at crossroads towards Benenden Hospital. Continue (WITH CAUTION) downhill past pond on left and then uphill, crossing a stile on the left just past a cottage. Cross diagonally towards the right through a field, leaving via a gate in top right-hand corner. Continue along a track between fences, pass through a gate and, bearing left, cross over the corner of a field. Cross a stile and proceed beside tennis courts.*

2. *Turn left and proceed along a tarmac driveway. Just before the main school building turn left through a gate and down a track. Cross a stile and turn right into a field in direction of a yellow arrow. Continue straight ahead (indicated by second arrow) to reach a stile in far right corner of field. Do not cross this stile, but bear left instead, proceeding downhill along border of same field. Cross stile in the bottom corner and then skirt border of playing field. Turn right and proceed to end of driveway.*

3. *Turn right into a road (B2086) (WITH CAUTION) and after about twenty yards turn left along indicated footpath between hedges. After about a hundred and fifty yards cross a stile on the left and then turn right, proceeding along right-hand border of a field. Cross another stile and continue downhill along right-hand border of a second field, passing through a small band of trees and beside a pond on the left. Pass through gate in bottom right-hand corner, continuing downhill along right-hand border of a third field. Pass through another gate.*

4. *Turn left along a track and then after a short distance pass through a gate. As track bears left proceed straight ahead uphill, following right border of a field. Continue along pathway between hedges. Climb a stile and cross a road (WITH CAUTION) to climb another stile opposite. Follow path diagonally towards the right through a field. Cross a stile and continue uphill into another field. Cross diagonally towards the right through this field. Pass through a kissing gate in top right corner and continue along tarmac footpath, bearing slightly right through a gate into a track. After about fifty yards turn right into a driveway and then left into a lane, proceeding downhill beside the green to reach The Street.*

61

---

old forest, the oak. From a lofty perch a carrion crow might suddenly launch itself into flight, its jarring cry mingling on the air with the lowing of cattle and the bleating of sheep, vigorously backed up by an orchestra of birdsong. In Spring children will be thrilled at the sight of little lambs playing hectic games of chase, either in the fields in front of the school or in one of many other rich green pastures along the way.

Having climbed the hedgerowed path up a hill from the old Roman road, the explorer will see the double oasts of Frame Farm over to the right before perhaps turning back for another look at the idyllic setting of Stream Farm in the valley below, with the white cowls of its oasts peeping through the trees.

The family may then enjoy seeing horses or perhaps a couple of friendly donkeys in the fields just before reaching the village green, where on occasion a game of cricket may be in progress in keeping with the fine old tradition, two local heroes of the 19th Century being Richard Mills and Edward Wenman who both played for the Kent Eleven.

Refreshments   At King William IV or The Bull public houses or a picnic on the route.

ROLVENDEN MILL

62

Rolvenden

Outline   Rolvenden ~ The Wilderness ~ Elphees ~ Rolvenden Mill ~
Rolvenden.

Summary   From behind the churchyard a wide panorama opens out
over undulating fields and clumps of woodland which slope towards the
Rother levels and the marsh beyond. It is difficult yet fascinating to
imagine that until the early 17th Century this outlook probably included
the sea, before the old estuary of the Rother near Appledore was blocked
and the river was diverted through a channel south of Oxney. With a fairy
well-proportioned mixture of open spaces and welcome, shady woods,
this walk may be an ideal choice on a hot, sunny day, although of course
for some tastes a touch of cloudy weather may do just as well, adding to
the dramatic atmosphere of the outing. Children can have fun trying to
keep count of the many rabbits in the fields, or perhaps join with their
parents in an appreciation of a wide variety of birds, butterflies and
wildflowers, including yellow buttercups, pink herb robert, white greater
stitchwort and tiny blue forget-me-nots. An unforgettable view of
Rolvenden Mill across the fields. also awaits as the route leads back
towards the tower of the church, visible ahead above the trees.

Attractions   A pink-breasted chaffinch singing from the branches of a
well-established oak near the church, sheep grazing in the lush green
pastures beyond, a pretty blue-tailed damsel fly, almost electric in a shaft
of sunlight, or a bee nosing through the wildflowers beneath a rich variety
of trees including silver birch, sweet chestnut, sycamore and ash, may all
combine to help the family leave their cares far behind as they stroll
across the fields and downhill between The Wilderness and the grounds
of Great Maytham Hall, which was once the home of Frances Hodgson
Burnett, author of Little Lord Fauntleroy. Peeping at lovely snippets of
the extensive gardens through the hedgerowed fence beside the
footpaths, parts of which are overhung with massive banks of
rhododendrons, the visitor may perhaps experience for themselves some
of the inspiration thought to have led to another of the author's books,
The Secret Garden.

On reaching a field the route turns right, although a pleasant
diversion may be made along a path to the left into Rolvenden Layne,
once a separate hamlet which later joined The Streyte, the settlement
near the church, to become the united village of Rolvenden.

continued on page 66

E

63

Route 15

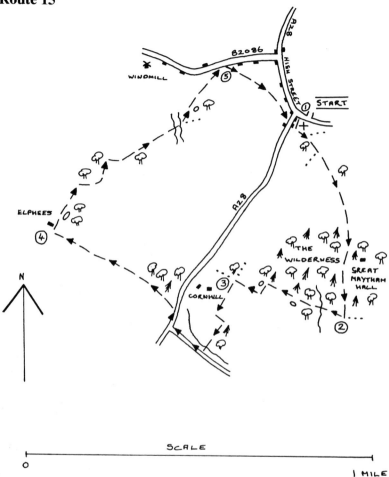

SCALE

0   1 MILE

64

Route 15

Rolvenden   3 miles

START   *at the church just off the High Street (O.S. Pathfinder 1250 G.R.845313). Parking in High Street (A28).*

ROUTE

1. *Enter churchyard through lych gate, passing war memorial on the right, before bearing left just past church. Keep to the right at a fork and leave churchyard via a kissing gate. Bearing left, cut through three fields before crossing a stile and following a path between fences through woods, passing grounds of Great Maytham Hall on the left.*

2. *Cross a stile and turn right, proceeding along border of a field. Cross another stile and continue downhill through trees. Cross footbridge and proceed uphill before climbing over another stile. Continue along right-hand border of two fields, crossing another stile between them. Cross another stile, turn left and then right, skirting the edge of a pond. Continue straight ahead into a field.*

3. *On reaching an oak tree in the middle of the field, turn left and after about a hundred yards cross a stile into another field. Continue straight ahead and cross a further stile. Turn left and then right, skirting the borders of a vineyard. Pass through a gate, cross a small bridge and turn right along a lane. On reaching the A28 turn right and proceed (WITH EXTREME CAUTION) for about fifty yards before turning left and passing through (or over) a gate. Proceed straight ahead along a path beside a fence, eventually passing through another gate. Continue along right border of a field. Pass through another gate and turn right, immediately passing through another gateway.*

4. *Follow path uphill, beside Elphees on the left and then a pond on the right before crossing over a stile directly ahead. Continue in direction of arrow along irregular left border of a field. After about two hundred yards cross over a stile in the far left corner (partially concealed by bushes!) and turn right, passing through a gateway. Cross diagonally towards the left through a large field. Cross a combination of a footbridge, a stile and then another footbridge in the far left corner, before turning left into another field. Pass through a wooden gateway directly ahead and then cross diagonally towards the right through another field.*

5. *Cross a strengthened section of fencing in far right corner of field (leading into a road) and then turn immediately right over a stile into another field. Cross diagonally towards the left through field. Proceed*

through a gap in a hedge and along left-hand border of school playing field. Cross a stile and continue along driveway, turning left into High Street and retracing steps to car.

ACCESS BY BUS
To Rolvenden from Ashford, Tenterden and Hastings.

———————

Continuing the walk, lovely views across the fields make an interesting change from the woods as the path runs beside a line of huge oaks, easily identifiable by their lobed, narrow leaves, and also sections of coppiced hornbeams, distinctly recognisable by their thick layers of serrated, oval-shaped leaves with ridged surfaces, as well as their grey, twisted or curling trunks and branches which go black when wet, a beautiful contrast with the green of the foliage.

The route then passes behind the quaint converted oast house of Cornhill and then later past the ideally situated Elphees. More fields and stiles follow (some of the stiles being rather high on this walk!) although the sudden, wonderful sight of the privately-owned Rolvenden Mill may well make one or two Tommy Steele fans break out into song, for this was the mill featured in the musical Half A Sixpence, the 1967 screen adaptation of Kipps, written by H. G. Wells. Such nostalgic exuberance may amuse the children, although the impressive mill itself, restored in 1956 as a memorial to a local lad, John Nicholas Barham, will be sure to command a fitting sense of awe and respect.

Children and adults alike might then enjoy a visit to the C. M. Booth Motor Museum in the High Street, perhaps before an ice cream from the general store, possibly an ideal way to complete the adventure.

Refreshments At the Star Inn or the Bull public house or perhaps a picnic along the way.

Tenterden

Outline Tenterden ~ Pittlesden Manor Farm ~ Coombe Farm ~ Grange Road ~ Tenterden.

Summary A strong sensation of stepping back in time may be felt at the quaint level crossing beside the platform of the Kent and East Sussex Railway, especially when the line is open, most weekends and various days of the week, with the sound of the whistle blowing and the chuff-chuff of the engine as the wheels begin to turn. From across the fields in the beautiful Chennell Park, during the early part of the walk, the carriages of the train might be seen away to the left, snaking slowly around the lush green hillside, an occasional plume of smoke heralding its advance. Youngsters will enjoy crossing fences, stiles and ingenious footbridges, while parents can savour a series of striking views including the picturesque double oasts of Potts Farm, the tranquil pond beside the driveway of Coombe Farm, the soaring spire of St. Michael's Church, seen in the distance from a peaceful and beautiful stretch of Grange Road, once part of a Roman trade route linking Canterbury and East Sussex, and then also the enormous tower of St. Mildred's Church from the footpath leading back through more rich farmland to the station.

Attractions Of course the bygone days of Tenterden go back a lot further than the age of the steam train which arrived in 1900, running twenty-one miles between Headcorn and Robertsbridge. Like many other Wealden towns the settlement began as a Saxon "den", a clearing in the forest where pigs were fed. Since then Tent-ware-den, as it was known to its next occupiers, the men of Thanet, has always enjoyed prosperity, its agricultural industry boosted with the introduction of sheep and the reclaiming of part of the Romney Marshes, before benefitting greatly from the growing cloth industry in the 13th Century and then being granted a charter by King Henry VI in the 15th Century, making the Town and Hundred of Tenterden a member of the Confederation of the Cinque Ports. In those days Tenterden was by the sea and was a handy neighbour to help the port of Rye fulfil its obligations in making ships for the navy.

Although the maritime trade slipped away in the 17th Century, more of the marshes became available as grazing land in the 18th Century and the cultivation of hops and fruit on the higher ground helped to play a part

continued on page 70

Route 16

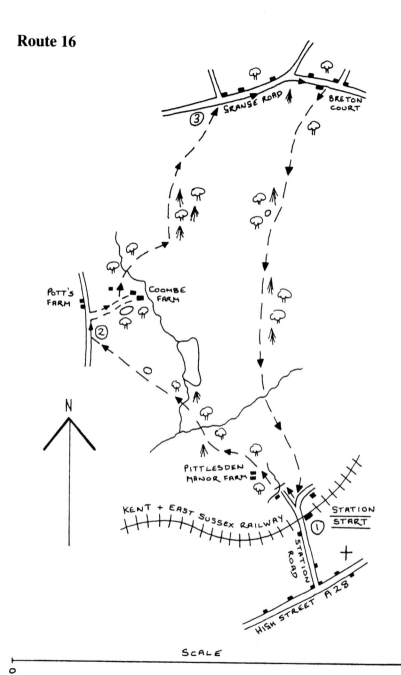

SRANSE ROAD

BRETON COURT

③

POTT'S FARM

COOMBE FARM

②

N

PITTLESDEN MANOR FARM

KENT + EAST SUSSEX RAILWAY

STATION START

①

STATION ROAD

HIGH STREET A28

SCALE

0

1 MILE

Route 16
Tenterden

3 miles

START   *at Tenterden Town Station (Kent and East Sussex Railway) at the bottom of Station Road (O.S. Pathfinder 1250 G.R.882335), approached by High Street (A28). Parking in town or at station.*

ROUTE

1. *From station proceed over level crossing and then downhill along left border of car park. At the bottom of the hill turn left over a footbridge and then right, following a winding path. Cross a stile and, bearing right, proceed along the border of a field. Continue downhill before crossing a footbridge with a stile at either end. Bearing slightly left, follow a path through another field, continuing over the brow of a hill before crossing another footbridge. Follow path uphill, passing through a kissing gate, before continuing uphill along left border of a field.*

2. *Cross a stile and turn right into a lane. After a hundred yards turn right and continue along driveway of Coombe Farm. Cross a stile to the left and proceed through a field in direction of arrows, leaving via a stile in far right corner, immediately followed by a footbridge. Bearing slightly left, continue uphill through a field. Cross stile in far left corner and proceed uphill along right border of another field, continuing straight ahead through a further section of same field. Cross stile and proceed diagonally towards the right through another field.*

3. *Pass through a gate and turn right along Grange Road. After about a quarter of a mile (just past Breton Court) turn right along indicated footpath between fences, eventually crossing over a stile. Follow a track along left border of a field. Cross a stile and follow path along right border of another field. Cross over section of strengthened fencing between two gates and follow path along right border of yet another field. Cross another stile and continue through another field. Cross a stile in the far left corner and continue downhill through another field. Cross a stile, then a footbridge and proceed uphill along a path, crossing a further stile to reach the station car park.*

ACCESS BY BUS
To Tenterden from Tunbridge Wells, Maidstone, Ashford and Hastings.

in making the town a successful market centre. In 1846 the railway line had reached as far as Headcorn, strengthening trade with London.

So many centuries of economic success are clearly, yet tastefully in evidence with a host of lovely old buildings in the town. The nearest to the route include St. Mildred's Church with its tower made of Bethersden marble, the Woolpack Hotel and also the former 16th Century Grammar School, a Wealden hall house, now The Man's Shop, all protected by the County Structure Plan which makes development restraint and conservation of paramount importance.

While some visitors will be satisfied to stroll through this delightful town, or perhaps take a wonderful ride on the train, others may feel quite rightly that there is also a great wealth to be appreciated in the surrounding countryside. The openness of the gently rolling farmland has its own undeniable appeal, with far-reaching views across the fields which are dotted with grazing animals and a treasure of well-established trees, a particularly lovely sight being the profuse pink blossom in June of a group of horse chestnuts straight ahead on the route at the top of a slope in Chennell Park.

For children the sight of sheep, cattle and horses will add to the fun, while parents might stop for a closer look at an impressive variety of wildflowers along the way, both in Spring and also in Summer when beautiful foxgloves stand tall beside the paths, showers of lesser stitchwort seem like little stars in the grass and the delicate petals of the stridently-coloured yellow and reddish birdsfoot trefoil hug the grassy slopes beside some of the hedgerows, their more popular name of "eggs and bacon" sure to raise a laugh!

Refreshments A variety of charming pubs and tea rooms in Tenterden.

HERB ROBERT
(pink April - October)

HURRAH FOR BODIAM CASTLE !

Appendices

ROUTES IN ORDER OF DIFFICULTY
Starting with the easiest:
Route 3 — *Wellington Rocks & Toad Rock - 3 miles*
Route 12 — *Hawkhurst - 2½ miles*
Route 16 — *Tenterden - 3 miles*
Route 14 — *Benenden - 3 miles*
Route 9 — *Lamberhurst - 3½ miles*
Route 2 — *Ashurst - 3½ miles*
Route 15 — *Rolvenden - 3 miles*
Route 10 — *Goudhurst - 2½ miles*
Route 7 — *Burwash - 3½ miles*
Route 1 — *Poohsticks Bridge - 4 miles*
Route 13 — *Bodiam Castle - 4 miles*
Route 11 — *Cranbrook - 4 miles*
Route 5 — *Rotherfield - 4 miles*
Route 4 — *Frant - 7 miles*
Route 8 — *Wadhurst - 4½ miles*
Route 6 — *Mayfield - 3½ miles*

PUBLIC TRANSPORT IN THE WEALD OF KENT AND SUSSEX
The area covered by this book is fairly well serviced by public transport although careful study of timetables is essential since some services tend to be infrequent.
For details of operators and timetables contact the following:
Boro'line Maidstone .... Tel. 0622 690060
British Rail .... Tel. 071 928 5100
Bygone Buses (Staplehurst) .... Tel. 0580 893680
Eagle Coaches .... Tel. 0892 24282
East Kent Road Car Company .... Tel. 0233 620344
East Sussex Rider Services .... Tel. 0273 478007
Kent County Council .... Tel. 0622 671411
(Highways & Transportation)
Kentish Bus .... Tel. 0474 321300
Lewes Bus Station .... Tel. 0273 474441
Maidstone & District .... Tel. 0634 847334
Tonbridge Bus Station .... Tel. 0732 356693
Tunbridge Wells Bus Station .... Tel. 0892 520221
Wealden Beeline (Tonbridge) .... Tel. 0892 833830

TOURIST INFORMATION CENTRES IN THE WEALD OF KENT AND SUSSEX
Ashford, Lower High Street. Tel. 0233 629165.
Battle, 88 High Street. Tel. 04246 3721.
Cranbrook, Vestry Hall, Stone Street. Tel. 0580 712538.
Maidstone, The Gatehouse, Mill Street. Tel. 0622 602169.
Rye, Strand Quay. Tel. 0797 226696.
Sevenoaks, Buckhurst Lane. Tel. 0732 450305.
Tenterden, Town Hall. Tel. 05806 3572.
Tunbridge Wells, Monson Way. Tel. 0892 515675.

WET WEATHER ALTERNATIVES IN THE WEALD OF KENT AND SUSSEX
completely or partly under cover.

It is advisable to check times of opening before a visit is made.

MUSEUMS AND CRAFT WORKSHOPS

A Day At The Wells, Tunbridge Wells, Tel. 0892 546545; highly imaginative guided tour through re-created scenes of high society in 1740. Special commentary for children. Open all year.

Ashford Museum, Ashford, Tel. 0233 621671; local history museum housed in Dr. Wilks' Hall, formerly the 17th Century Grammar School. Open Tuesdays and Saturdays all year.

Brattle Farm Museum, Staplehurst, Tel. 0580 891222; working farm with agricultural museum. Open April to October.

C. M. Booth Museum, Rolvenden, Tel. 0580 241234; collection of historic vehicles. Display includes ten Morgans. Open Mondays to Saturdays.

Ellen Terry Memorial Museum, Tenterden, Tel. 05806 2334; National Trust museum. Open afternoons except Thursdays and Fridays.

Finchcocks Living Museum of Music, Goudhurst, Tel. 0580 211702; noted collection of well-preserved historical keyboard instruments displayed in early Georgian house with gardens and parkland. Concerts and musical tours. Open April to September. Refreshments.

Frank Berry Pottery, Hildenborough, Tel. 0732 832225; visitors invited to watch earthenware and stoneware pots being made. Oast house models are also a speciality. Open all year Tuesdays to Saturdays.

Haxted Mill, near Edenbridge, Tel. 0732 862914; working mill on the River Eden and museum with fascinating displays including working models and slides accompanied by recorded commentaries. Also exhibition of the iron industry in the Weald. Open: April to May, Bank Holidays and weekends, June to September, afternoons.

Maidstone Museum and Art Gallery, Maidstone, Tel. 0622 754497; a wide range of displays to suit all ages. Open all year.

Museum of Kent Rural Life, Sandling, Tel. 0622 763936; informative displays on hop farming, including tools and machinery. Working oast house. Calendar of special events. Open Easter to October.

Pooks Hill Toy Museum, Burwash Weald, Tel. 0435 882072; private collection of toys from turn of the century to present day displayed in old Victorian shop. Open April to September.

Quarry Steam Museum, Bodiam, Tel. 0580 830670; exhibition of privately-owned steam engines. Open May to October.

Stocks Mill, near Tenterden, Tel. 0797 270537; post mill built in 1781 and later fully restored. Museum. Open June to September.

Tenterden Museum, Tenterden, Tel. 05806 4310; exhibitions and presentations of local history. Open afternoons daily from April to October.

Toy and Model Museum, Lamberhurst, Tel. 0892 890711; entertaining model museum. Open all year.

Tunbridge Wells Museum and Art Gallery, Tunbridge Wells, Tel. 0892 526121; displays and exhibitions including toys and dolls. Open Mondays to Saturdays.

CASTLES, HOUSES AND CHURCHES

Bateman's, Burwash, Tel. 0435 882302; Rudyard Kipling's home between 1902 and 1936. Display of his rooms and study; working water mill and gardens. Open April to October.

Bodiam Castle, near Robertsbridge, Tel. 0580 830436; 14th Century castle erected to block the Rother Valley as a defence against a feared invasion by the French. Excellent views from some of the towers. Open April to October.

Scotney Castle Garden, Lamberhurst, Tel. 0892 890651; remains of 14th Century castle with surrounding gardens. Open April to November.

Sheffield Park Garden, near Uckfield, Tel. 0825 790655; garden designed in 18th Century with five split-level lakes and display of rare trees and shrubs. Open April to November.

Sissinghurst Castle Garden, near Cranbrook, Tel. 0580 712850; creation of Vita Sackville West, including orchard, spring and herb garden. Open April to October.

More information on the above can be obtained from the National Trust.

Allington Castle, Allington, Tel. 0622 754080; moated castle with exhibition of art and furniture. Open all year.

Bayham Abbey, Lamberhurst, Tel. 0892 890381; Teise Valley remains of 13th Century abbey owned by monks between 1208 and 1525. Open April to September.

Bentley Estate, near Lewes, Tel. 0825 840573; Tudor farmhouse with collection of furniture and paintings. Also collection of vintage cars, gardens, tearoom, picnic and play area with miniature steam railway. Open daily March to October.

Boughton Monchelsea Place, Boughton Monchelsea, Tel. 0622 743120; Elizabethan manor house built of Kentish ragstone in 1567. Exhibitions of items from clothes to farm implements. Views over deer park. Open Easter to October. Refreshments.

Brickwall House and Gardens, Northiam, Tel. 0797 223329; beautiful gardens with 18th Century bowling alley, sunken topiary garden and chess garden. Open April to September.

Chiddingstone Castle, near Edenbridge, Tel. 0892 870347; former seat of the Streatfields, converted to a castle in about 1805. Special attractions include: The Royal Stuart and Jacobite Collections, Japanese Art, Armour and Swords, Egyptian Antiquities and Buddhist Art. Open end of March to September.

Godinton House and Garden, Ashford, Tel. 0233 620773; mainly Jacobean house noted for its fine carving and panelling. Displays of porcelain and furniture. 18th Century garden including topiary. Open April to September.

Great Dixter House and Gardens, Northiam, Tel. 0797 253160; 15th Century manor house with great hall restored by Sir Edward Lutyens, who also designed the attractive gardens. Open April to October. Refreshments.

Great Maytham Hall, Rolvenden, Tel. 0580 241346; walled garden, house designed by Sir Edward Lutyens, formerly the home of novelist Frances Hodgson Burnett. Open Wednesday and Thursday afternoons, May to September.

Hammerwood Park, near Forest Row, Tel. 0342 850594; lovingly restored building with displays of furniture, costumes and agricultural implements. Open April to September. Refreshments.

Hever Castle, near Edenbridge, Tel. 0732 865224; 13th Century castle and ornamental gardens, once the home of Anne Boleyn. Open end of March to November afternoons only.

Haremere Hall, Etchingham, Tel. 058081 245; Tudor manor house with terraced gardens including nature trail and picnic site. Refreshments. Ring for details of opening.

Leeds Castle, near Maidstone, Tel. 0622 765400; medieval castle and gardens with aviary. Open April to October daily and November to March weekends only.

Marle Place Gardens, Brenchley, near Tonbridge, Tel. 089272 2304; nursery and gardens with ponds and woodland walks. Gardens open Wednesdays only, nursery daily April to October.

Owl House Gardens, Lamberhurst, Tel. 0892 890230; 16th Century cottage used by wool smugglers, with walks through gardens noted for their rhododendrons, azaleas, roses and ornamental fruit trees. Ring for details of opening.

Penshurst Place, Penshurst, Tel. 0892 870307; medieval hall built in 1340 with 15th Century extensions retaining their Gothic character. Former residence of kings and dukes surrounded by Tudor-inspired gardens. Also, Venture Playground and Toy Museum. Open April to October, daily except Mondays.

Tonbridge Castle, Tonbridge High Street, Tel. 0732 770929 (Tourist Information Centre); Norman Castle with 13th Century gatehouse. Gardens and grounds with views of the Medway. Open daily.

All Saints Church, Hawkhurst (Highgate), designed by Sir George Gilbert Scott and built with local sandstone in 1861.

Church of St. Alban, Frant, 15th Century church, rebuilt in 1819.

Church of King Charles The Martyr, Tunbridge Wells, extended chapel built in 1678, with ceiling work by Henry Doogood who was the chief plasterer to Sir Christopher Wren.

Church of St. Denys, Rotherfield, built on same site as original church founded by Berhtwald, a Saxon duke, in 792 A.D.

Church of St. Dunstan, Cranbrook, medieval church, known as the Cathedral of the Weald.

Church of St. Martin, Ashurst, built between 921 and 927 A.D. and since restored several times.

Church of St. Mary, Goudhurst, 14th Century church, housing monuments to the Culpeper family.

Church of St. Mary, Lamberhurst, 13th Century church, with wall tablet commemorating Christopher Hussey (1899-1970).

Parish Church of St. Laurence, Hawkhurst (The Moor), built in 1350 during the reign of King Edward III, with turreted west tower.

St. Bartholomew's Church, Burwash, 12th Century tower, former curates including the poet, Rev. James Hurdis, and Victorian writer, Rev. John Coker.

St. Dunstan's Church, Mayfield, 13th Century church, rebuilt in 15th Century. Erected on same site as the original wooden one built by St. Dunstan, Archbishop of Canterbury from 960 to 988 A.D.

St. George's Church, Benenden, rebuilt in 1678 after being struck by lightning. Further restored in 1862.

St. Giles Church, Bodiam, early 13th Century, with low perpendicular lancet window and nave roof extending over aisles.

St. Mary the Virgin Church, Rolvenden, 14th Century stone church with existing gallery and pew made in 1825.

St. Mildred's Church, Tenterden, part 13th Century with stained glass window depicting St. Mildred, Abbess of Minster.

St. Pauls's Church, Rusthall, built using local sandstone in 1849, with huge central tower.

St. Peter & St. Paul Church, Wadhurst, with thirty iron grave-slabs embedded in the floor, dating from 1617 to 1790.

TRAINS, FARMS, VINEYARDS AND WILDLIFE ATTRACTIONS

Ashdown Forest Farm, Wych Cross, Tel. 082571 2040; Survival Centre approved by the Rare Breeds Survival Trust for endangered species not usually found on modern farms. Special calendar of events from lambing and ploughing to rural crafts and sheep-shearing. Refreshments at farm shop or picnic with view over Ashdown Forest. Open daily except Christmas.

Badsell Park Farm, Matfield, Tel. 0892 832549; pet area and animal farm. Also pick your own fruit, nature trail and bird and insect displays. Open May to November. Refreshments. Picnic site.

Barnsgate Manor Vineyards, Uckfield, Tel. 082571 3366; ring for details of tours, meals and winetasting.

Bartley Mill, Bell's Yew Green, Tel. 0892 890372; formerly a hop farm, now milling organic wheat. Craft shop, museum and farm trail. Open all year except Christmas period. Refreshments and picnic site.

Bedgebury National Pinetum, Goudhurst, Tel. 0580 211044; renowned collection of conifers owned by the Forestry Commission with a lake and two streams. Trail indicated by arrows and listening posts. Open April to September.

Bewl Water, Lamberhurst, Tel. 0892 890661; lakeside walk, picnic sites and adventure playground. Open all year. Refreshments.

Biddenden Vineyards, Biddenden, Tel. 0580 291726; ring for details of tours, meals and winetasting.

Bluebell Railway Operating Ltd., Uckfield, Tel. 082572 3777; steam railway rides between Sheffield Park and Horsted Keynes. Open all year except Christmas and Boxing Day.

Caxton Tonbridge Waterways, Tonbridge, Tel. 0732 456918; cruises along the River Medway. Open Easter to September.

Cranbrook Union Windmill, Cranbrook, Tel. 0580 712256; working mill thought to be one of the largest in the country, once owned by a union of local tradesmen. Open April to September.

Drusillas Park, Alfriston, Tel. 0323 870234; zoo, adventure playground, rail tour through animal paddocks, a variety of craft, gift and toy shops, with refreshment facilities including playland food bar, pub, snackbar and restaurant. Open all year except Christmas and Boxing Day.

Five Chimneys Vineyards, Uckfield, Tel. 082581 3159; ring for details of tours, meals and winetasting.

Flimwell Bird Park, Flimwell, Tel. 0580 87202; exotic waterfowl, swans, pheasants, 14 acres of woodland, children's playground, picnic area and refreshments bar. Open March to September.

Great Knelle Farm, Rye, Tel. 0797 260321; conducted tractor train tour of rare animal breed farm, adventure playground, fishing, craft shops, picnic area and refreshments bar. Open April to October.

Heaven Farm, Uckfield, Tel. 0825 790177; nature trail and museum with guided tours. Open all year. Refreshments.

High Rocks, Tunbridge Wells, Tel. 0892 515532; historic monument of sandstone outcrops. Open all year. Ring for times.

Hollanden Farm Park, Hildenborough, Tel. 0732 832276; collection of rare farm animals, display of antique farming equipment, Iron Age settlement and adventure playground. Open: Easter to October. Refreshments.

Iden Croft Herb Farm & Garden, Staplehurst, Tel. 0580 891432; aromatic herb gardens, including National Oreganium Collection. Also garden for the blind and disabled. Open all year.

Kent & East Sussex Steam Railway, Tenterden, Tel. 05806 5155; steam railway rides from Tenterden to Northiam. Open Easter to Dec. (check for days of opening).

Lamberhurst Vineyards, Lamberhurst, Tel. 0892 890844; vineyard trail and winetasting. Farm shop. Open all year. Refreshments.

Lavender Line Steam Museum, Isfield, near Uckfield, Tel. 082575 515; rides on vintage steam train with museum and buffet coach. Open March to December.

Merrydown Wine, near Heathfield, Tel. 04353 2254; tours through cider and winemaking factory. Open Tuesday to Friday, Easter to October.

Tenterden Vineyards, Tenterden, Tel. 05806 3033; ring for details of tours, meals and winetasting.

The Sussex Shire Horses, Etchingham, Tel. 058081 501; home of thirty horses including Shires, Suffolk Punches, Ardennes, Cart Horses and Heavy Work Cobs. Demonstrations and presentations with a view to promoting conservation and care for the environment. Open daily July to September.

Whitbread Hop Farm, Beltring, Paddock Wood, Tel. 0622 872068; working hop farm with museum, craft centre, children's play area and pets corner. Open Easter to October. Refreshments.

SPORTING FACILITIES

Angel Centre, Tonbridge, Tel. 0732 359966.

Bewl Watersports, Bewl, Tel. 0892 890661.

Cranbrook & District Swimming Pool, Cranbrook, Tel. 0580 714695.

Edenbridge Leisure Centre, Edenbridge, Tel. 0732 865665.

Kings Leisure Centre, East Grinstead, Tel. 0342 328616.

Lido, Tonbridge, Tel. 0732 355061.

Sports and 'Y' Centre, Tunbridge Wells, Tel. 0892 540744.

Stour Centre, Ashford, Tel. 0233 639966.

Tenterden Leisure Centre, Tenterden, Tel. 05806 5987.

BIBLIOGRAPHY

Alan Bignell, Kent Villages, 1975.

Peter Brereton, Touring Guide to English Villages, 1984.

Jim Cleland, The Visitor's Guide to Sussex, 1985.

Henry S. Eeles, Frant: a parish history, 1947.

Roger Higham, Kent, 1974.

Sheila Kaye-Smith, Weald of Kent and Sussex, 1973.

Kevin MacDonnell, A Photographer's Guide to Kent, 1986.

Kev Reynolds, The Visitor's Guide to Kent, 1990.

Warden Swinfen & David Arscott, BBC Radio Sussex Guide to Hidden Sussex, 1984.

The Vanguard Rambling Club, The Vanguard Way, 1980.

Rev. A. C. White, Ashurst: notes on the history, 1955.

Patricia Wright, Frant: the story of a Wealden parish, 1982.

THE FAMILY WALKS SERIES

Family Walks on Anglesey. Laurence Main	ISBN 0 907758 66 5
Family Walks in Berkshire & North Hampshire. Kathy Sharp	ISBN 0 907758 37 1
Family Walks around Bristol, Bath & the Mendips. Nigel Vile	ISBN 0 907758 19 3
Family Walks around Cardiff & the Valleys. Gordon Hindess	ISBN 0 907758 54 1
Family Walks in Cheshire. Chris Buckland	ISBN 0 907758 29 0
Family Walks in Cornwall. John Caswell	ISBN 0 907758 55 X
Family Walks in the Cotswolds. Gordon Ottewell	ISBN 0 907758 15 0
Family Walks in the Dark Peak. Norman Taylor	ISBN 0 907758 16 9
Family Walks in East Sussex. Sally & Clive Cutter	ISBN 0 907758 71 1
Family Walks on Exmoor & the Quantocks. John Caswell	ISBN 0 907758 46 0
Family Walks in Gower. Amanda Green	ISBN 0 907758 63 0
Family Walks in Hereford and Worcester. Gordon Ottewell	ISBN 0 907758 20 7
Family Walks on the Isle of Wight. Laurence Main	ISBN 0 907758 56 8
Family Walks in the Lake District. Barry McKay	ISBN 0 907758 40 1
Family Walks in Mendip, Avalon & Sedgemoor. Nigel Vile	ISBN 0 907758 41 X
Family Walks in Mid Wales. Laurence Main	ISBN 0 907758 27 4
Family Walks in the New Forest. Nigel Vile	ISBN 0 907758 60 6
Family Walks in the North Wales Borderlands. Gordon Emery	ISBN 0 907758 50 9
Family Walks North West Kent. Clive Cutter	ISBN 0 907758 36 3
Family Walks in the North Yorkshire Dales. Howard Beck	ISBN 0 907758 52 5
Family Walks in Oxfordshire. Laurence Main	ISBN 0 907758 38 X
Family Walks in Pembrokeshire. Laurence Main	ISBN 0 907758 75 4
Family Walks in Snowdonia. Laurence Main	ISBN 0 907758 32 0
Family Walks in South Derbyshire. Gordon Ottewell	ISBN 0 907758 61 4
Family Walks around the South Downs. Nick Channer	ISBN 0 907758 73 8
Family Walks in South Gloucestershire. Gordon Ottewell	ISBN 0 907758 33 9
Family Walks in South Shropshire. Marian Newton	ISBN 0 907758 30 4
Family Walks in South Yorkshire. Norman Taylor	ISBN 0 907758 25 8
Family Walks in the Staffordshire Peak & Potteries. Les Lumsdon	ISBN 0 907758 34 7
Family Walks around Stratford & Banbury. Gordon Ottewell	ISBN 0 907758 49 5
Family Walks in Suffolk. C.J. Francis	ISBN 0 907758 64 9
Family Walks in Surrey. Norman Bonney	ISBN 0 907758 74 6
Family Walks around Swansea. Raymond Humphreys	ISBN 0 907758 62 2
Family Walks in the Teme Valley. Camilla Harrison	ISBN 0 907758 45 2
Family Walks in Three Peaks & Malham. Howard Beck	ISBN 0 907758 42 8
Family Walks in Warwickshire. Geoff Allen	ISBN 0 907758 53 3
Family Walks in the Weald of Kent & Sussex. Clive Cutter	ISBN 0 907758 51 7
Family Walks in West London. Caroline Bacon	ISBN 0 907758 72 X
Family Walks in West Yorkshire. Howard Beck	ISBN 0 907758 43 6
Family Walks in the White Peak. Norman Taylor	ISBN 0 907758 09 6
Family Walks in Wiltshire. Nigel Vile	ISBN 0 907758 21 5
Family Walks in the Wye Valley. Heather & John Hurley	ISBN 0 907758 26 6

The publishers welcome suggestions for further titles in this series; and will be pleased to consider manuscripts relating to Derbyshire from new or established authors.

Scarthin Books of Cromford, in the Peak District, are also leading second-hand and antiquarian booksellers, and are eager to purchase specialised material, both ancient and modern.

Contact Dr D.J. Mitchell, 0629-823272.